THE GREEN
IMPERATIVE

Celebrating Forty Years of *Resurgence* Magazine

www.resurgence.org

First published in *Resurgence* Magazine,
Ford House, Hartland, Bideford, Devon EX39 6EE
www.resurgence.org

This edition is published by Resurgence Books

Edited by Lorna Howarth, Satish Kumar and
Sophie Poklewski Koziell

ISBN 978 1 900322 23 2

Designed and set by Simon Willby

Printed in England by ImprintDigital.net

WELCOME
SATISH KUMAR

ENVIRONMENTAL NARRATIVES

*R*ESURGENCE IS A CHILD of the sixties. Rachel Carson's *Silent Spring* came out in 1962 and alerted us to the plight of the Earth. At that time I was walking with a friend from India to Moscow, Paris, London and Washington for peace. I soon realised that unless we make peace with the Earth there can be no peace among humans.

E. F. Schumacher, Leopold Kohr, John Seymour and Barbara Ward were all thinking on the same wavelength but it fell upon John Papworth, who walked with me in the USA, to conceive the idea of a forum which would bring together all the great thinkers and activists of that time. Thus *Resurgence* was born.

When John and I walked together in the streets and neighbour-hoods of the American cities we heard the songs of John Lennon, Joan Baez and Bob Dylan. We participated in the protests against the Vietnam War, we joined the Civil Rights marchers led by Martin Luther King in Albany and Atlanta and we talked about a holistic worldview in which humanity and the Earth are in harmony.

Soon after *Resurgence* was launched in 1966, Edward (Teddy) Goldsmith started *The Ecologist* and published *A Blueprint for Survival*, which inspired and activated a whole generation of civil society.

In 1972 Teddy and I went to Stockholm for the first ever UN conference on the environment. There, *Limits to Growth* was launched and a new energy was unleashed which was felt around the world.

While the *Blueprint* and *Limits* produced political awareness, E. F. Schumacher's *Small is Beautiful* gave a philosophical, spiritual and economic grounding to the environmental movement. It was at this time, in 1973, that my wife June and I accepted John Papworth's invitation to become editors of *Resurgence*. Fritz Schumacher gave his backing to my editorship by saying, "There are many Gandhians in India; we need one here in England." To which I countered, "I am prepared to edit if you agree to write in every issue." Which he did until his death in 1976.

Then, with the backing of *Resurgence* readers and contributors, the E. F. Schumacher Society, the Schumacher Lectures, the Small School, Green Books and eventually Schumacher College were established to carry on the work of bringing ecology, spirituality and social justice together.

While *Resurgence* grew slowly and steadily, the environmental movement went from strength to strength: Friends of the Earth, Greenpeace and a number of Green parties around the world became the platform for the millions of activists. Gaia Theory, Deep Ecology, Organic Farming, Self-Sufficiency, Back to the Land, Renewable Energy, Community Technology, Farmers' Markets, Vegetable Box Schemes, Permaculture, Bioregionalism and Localism were some of the expressions of a new ecological worldview, which the environmental movement championed and *Resurgence* magazine represented.

IN THE PAST forty years the paradigm has shifted. Now *The Independent* newspaper runs cover stories on the environment, arch consumer magazine *Vanity Fair* has produced a special issue proclaiming "Green is the New Black" and even the UK Conservative Party ran its local election campaign on the motto "Vote Blue, Get Green". These are signs of changing times which give us a cause for optimism. If the trend continues then the shift in political priorities and policies is bound to follow. But to make sure that they do, green groups and eco-activists have to join forces and work together. The past forty years have laid the foundations for a better future. Now we need to build on that foundation so that the coming generations have a sustainable future. The many groups of the environmental movement show strength in diversity but it is essential that, whatever single issue we are focusing on, we hold the big picture in our minds. The time has come when separate and disparate groups must stand together. Alone we are weak but together we are strong and we can change the world. I would like to see *Resurgence* representing the united voice of the environmental movement.

TO MARK OUR 40th anniversary we have published this special book, which asks many of our celebrated contributors to tell us their personal stories so that we know how they have contributed to the environmental narrative of the past forty years. So here we have some of the most inspiring tales which have shaped the thoughts and actions of a movement that is addressing the most urgent challenges of our time. May these stories stimulate our readers and inspire them to live well and act well.

Satish Kumar, editor, Resurgence magazine

WE'RE IN THIS TOGETHER

If we view the world as an interdependent global village, then we avoid taking action at our own peril.

WE LIVE IN complicated times. We seek, but we don't necessarily find, the ultimate things we long to experience - contentment, joy, love, inner peace. Our lives are too often overloaded with demands: that we should be successful, rich, beautiful and famous; but this just adds to our inner stress and turmoil. The media constantly bombard us with images reminding us of our 'lack' ... and we so often feel like failures.

Life's condition means that at any given moment the things we value most can be swiftly taken away from us. Our health, our safety and security, both emotionally and physically, cannot be guaranteed, so we carry our anxiety and fear of loss within and around us, unwittingly. We strive for a 'better moment' than the one we are currently in, while dragging the burdens of our past into every present situation, so that we are rarely, if ever, 'here and now'.

How do we find meaning, value and connection in a society that is dislocated and in many ways dysfunctional? We have lost our sense of community or belonging to anything much beyond our own individual circumstance. We have become voyeurs, vacuously gazing at reality TV shows and sitcoms while exhibitionists and ever-new 'celebrities' grab their shot at fifteen minutes of fame.

Technology has radically altered our existence in so many ways. Everything happens faster, while we struggle to keep up, ever desperate to be ahead of the game. In isolation we scan the internet, and email or text our friends, as a substitute for real connection. We inform ourselves about the soaring crime rate, the effects of drug and alcohol abuse, domestic violence, the horrors of war, the scandalous antics of corrupt corporate businessmen and their friends, the politicians.

We digest the endless details of humankind's abuse and exploitation, while our polluted planet heats up around us. Ice caps melt, ancient rainforests disappear, the population explodes and animal species hurtle towards extinction. I have therefore come to the conclusion that the world is completely and utterly mad! And perhaps I am mad to have any expectation that it could be anything otherwise. But somehow I still cling to the notion that there is some kind of intelligence, sanity, goodness, compassion, or hope, somewhere on this planet.

I HAVE A view of the world as an interdependent global village. We avoid taking action at our own peril. I would like to see the democratic voters of this country take a more active part in the social and political events that affect our lives, because we actually do have far more power than we ever seem to realise. We have freedom of speech and democracy, but we seem to become complacent once we've put a political party into power. I'd love to see Britain at the forefront of a visionary and exemplary response to the problems we all face. I had earnestly hoped to see something of that change over the last ten years of Labour government, but it seems, sadly, that this will not be delivered.

I don't believe that you can *ever* solve the problem of terrorism by acts of brutal retaliatory violence. I think the so-called war on terror is scandalous because it is a cover-up, and not a solution. It is in fact America's second Vietnam. I do not believe the Iraqi people are being liberated. They are being destroyed. I do not believe the planet can continue *ad infinitum* with our endless exploitation of its natural resources. I do not believe that human beings have *ever* created a political structure which works for the benefit of all, rather than the few.

We need to see more action to follow through from rhetoric. We need to see the noble ideals of justice and accountability put into action, before developing countries can ever begin to take any steps out of chronic and endemic poverty. I want to see an effective response to the genocide of AIDS that is decimating millions of people not only in Africa, but across the globe. Antiretroviral drugs extend and save people's lives: they must be made available. Yet in a country like South Africa, which has the highest instance of HIV/AIDS, there is still, unbelievably, a culture of denial, effectively preventing people getting access to treatment. Like terrorism and environmental disasters, AIDS has no boundaries. We are all in this together, whether we realise it or not.

WHEN RESURGENCE MAGAZINE first started, over forty years ago, there was no ecological or new age movement (well, there was, but they were called hippies!) There were few health food shops or alternative medical treatment centres. Nowadays the 'alternative' has actually evolved into something that is pretty much mainstream. Who would have guessed that supermarkets would have an organic food section, or market their products under 'green' auspices?

Positive change is happening, and we should be encouraged by this. But we cannot afford to become complacent. To me, 'green' actually means 'survival at every level' - it is not merely the current trendy consumer catchword. And 'green' needs to be continuously integrated into our daily lives.

I applaud all environmentalists, activists, radical freethinkers, writers, idealists, creators, philosophers, artists, students and teachers who challenge us to go against the grain, to question, to think, and to respond to the world outside the box: those who search for the truth behind a culture of lies and disinformation, who refuse to give in to pessimism in the face of what often seems like a lost cause.

That is why I love *Resurgence* ... and why I have the most profound respect for this inspirational magazine. I'm proud to be counted as one of the lunatic idealists ... who passionately endorse the notion of a better, safer, kinder world.

Annie Lennox is a singer and social activist.

CONTENTS

12   ROSAMUND KIDMAN-COX
WILDNESS AND FREEDOM

17   JERRY MANDER
EARTHQUAKES OF CONSCIOUSNESS

22   RICHARD MABEY
BIOLUXURIANCE

27   RICHARD HEINBERG
BEYOND PEAK OIL

31   DAVID NICHOLSON-LORD
THE GREAT URBAN INDOORS

36   MICHAEL MEACHER
WHITHER THE ENVIRONMENTAL MOVEMENT?

41   DAVID PEARSON
BUILDING A BETTER WORLD

46   JEREMY LEGGETT
FROM CARBON TO SOLAR

55   GEOFF MULGAN
THE ENEMY WITHIN

61   ANDREW SIMMS
RICHER? YES; HAPPIER? NO

68   ANITA RODDICK
BUCKING THE SYSTEM

74   DEEPAK CHOPRA
DISPELLING THE DARKNESS

78   PETER LANG
GREEN GENEROSITY

83	TIM SMIT
	IMAGINATION HOLDS THE KEY
90	JONATHON PORRITT
	EDGING CLOSER TO MELTDOWN
95	JOHN ELKINGTON
	THE BUSINESS END OF ALL THIS
101	CAROLINE LUCAS
	LOW-CARBON FUTURE
108	ALAN SIMPSON
	THE LONG AND WINDING ROAD
114	DAVID BOYLE
	IN SEARCH OF AUTHENTICITY
119	SARA PARKIN
	LESSONS ON LEADERSHIP
124	LINDSAY CLARKE
	REVALUING THE NOVEL
129	JAMES LOVELOCK
	MAKING PEACE WITH GAIA
138	PAUL ALLEN
	JOINING UP THE DOTS
143	SCILLA ELWORTHY
	INVESTING IN HEALING
149	FIONA REYNOLDS
	A RURAL REPLAN
154	FRITJOF CAPRA
	LEARNING FROM LEONARDO

A PASSIONATE PROPONENT
ROSAMUND KIDMAN-COX

WILDNESS AND FREEDOM

Most of the fields of my childhood
were built over.

I SPENT MY childhood in Devon, much of it rummaging around outside. My parents, having lived in the tropics, had a camping-out attitude to life. So I was left to my own devices, to roam at will.

My epiphany came at age seven when, pretending to be a horse, I took a blind jump over a bank onto an adder, which defended itself by striking. It hit the top of my gumboot, and the venom trickled down. Scared and angry, I killed it with a stick. Then I dissected it. Inside were pristine baby adders, each in a transparent birth bag - the most beautiful tiny creatures. I was filled with horror at what I had done but fascinated by what I had seen. From then on, nature became a passion.

Foraging for wild flowers in the lanes and bridleways was a favourite entertainment. On one such expedition, I met a real botanist, W. Keble Martin, who showed me the miniature flowers of fairy flax. I was hooked. Later, his book *The New Concise British Flora*, with basic text but the most beautiful paintings, would become a treasured possession.

The childhood gift I had was to learn from nature. That far fewer children can do this today is one of society's great losses. Primrose flowers were interesting because they could be divided into 'thrum' and 'pin' (tall and short stigmas) and were visited by bee-flies. But they were also things of beauty, with a delicate taste and aroma that conjured up warm spring sun. Only when you have an emotional connection with something do you really care what happens to it.

AT SCHOOL, I loved biology - as long as it involved drawing and finding out about things. But at university, the outdoor world was transformed into biochemistry and physics. Lectures involved little about ecology as I understood it - the relationships between all living things, including humans, and their environment - and nothing about ethics or conservation. Using electrodes to make the legs of a dissected frog twitch resulted merely in it jerking to life and flopping over the floor, needles and guts hanging out. And running currents through locusts to determine nerve lengths seemed more like pulling wings off flies. So I went on to study art and English, never having been able to divorce the arts from the sciences - and hoping to find a way to work with both.

Reading books by the naturalists, biologists and natural philosophers, from Peter Scott and Jane Goodall to Richard Dawkins and Richard Mabey, was what subsequently taught me more about the natural world. But my most profound education came in Borneo.

A botanical grant gave me a chance to travel to Sabah in the early 1970s. At that time, the majority of the country was rainforest; there were almost no cars and just one main road, in the capital. I saw raf-flesia, giant pitcher-plants, proboscis monkeys and orang-utans. But I also witnessed logging, the spread of oil-palm plantations and the bulldozing of a major road through the centre - the harshest illustration of the link between consumption and destruction and what gives rise to wealth and poverty, spiritual as well as material.

One day, when collecting in the forest, with the sound of chain-saws nearby, I heard the most terrifying noise: the groaning and renting of a great tree falling, pulling with it trunks and branches. The noise was so all-enveloping that it was impossible to tell in which direction the giant was falling and where to run to. When it came to earth, I saw what its canopy held - a garden of epiphytes and a community of animals, including an electric-blue earthworm. And when, on the flight back, I saw deforestation from the air - one of the ugliest of sights - and an orang-utan marooned in a tree left standing among chaos, I understood how fast the world could change. That same decade, rampant development also took hold in Devon, and most of the fields of my childhood were built over.

THE 1970s SAW an increase in natural history publications, which gave me my first publishing jobs. It also gave rise to the great television series *Life on Earth* in 1979, presenting biological diversity and its interconnectedness to a mass audience.

In 1981, I became Editor of *Wildlife* magazine (started in 1963, just after the founding of the World Wildlife Fund, now WWF) and just before the birth of *Resurgence*. Originally called *Animals*, its focus was on single-species conservation and simple enjoyment of other animals. Yet its launch issues serialised *Silent Spring*, Rachel Carson's landmark book on pesticide use. Over the past forty years or so, its content has charted the issues and changing paths of conservation.

In 1983, in line with the growth of nature as screen subject, the magazine transformed into BBC *Wildlife* and moved to Bristol, home of the BBC Natural History Unit. The 1980s were the heady days of campaigning, when Friends of the Earth and Greenpeace became high-profile. New arrivals on the scene included the Environmental Investigation Agency (EIA), with its single-focus, media-savvy campaigns, and the Born Free Foundation and the Whale and Dolphin Conservation Society, which, like the International Fund for Animal Welfare (IFAW), embraced both animal-welfare concerns and species conservation. All appealed to the public through gut emotions first.

But the focus of conservation was changing, marked by the Bruntland Report in 1987, with its mantra of sustainable development. And the gap was also widening between laypeople and value-led conservationists, and the conservationists who subscribed to economic rationalism - who presented nature as a commodity and didn't question the notion of development as a virtue. As conservation adopted the language of utilitarianism to forge closer relationships with government and business, so passion and emotion became regarded as irresponsible. The flaw of such a view is, of course, that any part of biodiversity which can't be justified in utilitarian terms - fairy flax for certain - gets thrown out of the ark. It also risks alienating those non-professionals motivated by passion.

I found myself searching out others who felt uneasy about corporate conservation - who didn't necessarily believe that poverty alleviation meant just wealth creation or that ethical, spiritual and aesthetic human needs were luxuries.

It's tempting just to say that, despite the growth in the number of conservation camps and the development of their expertise, conservation will never keep pace with the development movement, that the capacity for self-deception and exploitation will always be with us and that the human population will continue to grow and consume more. Certainly, the problems covered in the magazine I worked on - tiger poaching, deforestation and over-fishing, for example - are as urgent now as they were twenty years ago. But then conservation will always be a matter of trying to hold a position, and only rarely does it manage to balance losses with creative restoration.

RECENT NATURAL AND unnatural disasters and a growing culture of fear have suddenly put conservation and environmental concerns in the media spotlight and linked them to human survival. We also now have the information-technology tools to collate vast amounts of information about the environment, share and access it in an instant, analyse what's happening and call for action. We know that it is possible to cut our consumption and reduce if not remove most human-made sources of climate change without serious impact on our quality of life. The difficulty for most of us is now not lack of understanding but altering everyday behaviour.

The key is re-evaluating what constitutes a good life. Values and emotions determine the decisions we make, and once we've recognised what we truly value, sustainable living becomes an inviting and vote-winning option.

What we need, desperately, are knowledgeable, articulate, popular and passionate proponents of life values and ecological sustainability - natural leaders who believe that wildlife belongs to everyone and to no-one, that wildness is essential for true freedom and that, for a child, experiencing the joy of nature at first hand is the most valuable education of all.

Rosamund Kidman Cox, former editor of BBC Wildlife Magazine, is now a freelance editor and writer specialising in nature and our relationship with the environment.

THE PARADIGM WARRIOR
JERRY MANDER

EARTHQUAKES
OF CONSCIOUSNESS

How I moved from advertising glitz
to anti-globalisation fervour.

I F ONE SEEKS revelatory moments to explain sharp turns in life,
then this was one for me. It was in 1964, during one of many mar-
tini-drinking evenings with David Brower, the late inspirational
leader of the Sierra Club, at New York's Biltmore Hotel, where he
often held court. Between drinks we discussed an advertising series
he had asked me to help write and design, opposing new mega-
dams being planned for the Grand Canyon.

I was in the commercial advertising business at that time, fulfilling an ambition from childhood. I was excited to be able to speak
imagery into the brains of millions of people and see them react as
we wanted. Of course, in passing, I was also seeing how these fabu-

lous new technologies of mental invasion were slowly bringing a global homogenisation of commodity consciousness. But I did not yet see much of a problem with that.

Brower's assignment was difficult. Las Vegas interests had been pushing for big dams to provide electricity to expand into the south-western desert. Congress was poised to authorise them. Desperate measures were required, Brower said. These dams would submerge hundreds of miles of wilderness river gorges, leaving lakes as much as a mile deep. The strata of those magnificent canyon walls, formed over billions of years, displayed the geologic history of the world. Equally important, Brower said, was that the experience of being in those canyons put people in touch with creation, and projected their consciousness back to the roots of existence. Drowning the canyons for corporate profits, during a brief one-century blip of geologic time since the industrial revolution, he said, would be an outrage to nature, to human consciousness, and to God.

The developers of the dams said the lakes would be a great thing, since they would encourage tourists in power-boats to get higher up the canyon walls for a closer look. So, the first ad of the series was headlined "Should We Flood the Sistine Chapel So Tourists Can Get Nearer the Ceiling?" That ad, and several that followed, produced tens of thousands of written letters to Congress. The dams were halted. Stewart Udall, then Secretary of the Interior under President Johnson, praised the ad campaign, calling it the first projection of a new modern environmental movement.

The ad series also projected me right out of the commercial advertising business. I finally understood that using the most pow-erful mentally invasive instruments on Earth to trivialise and com-modify existence was not such an ideal calling. I closed the commer-cial ad agency and started a new non-profit company that worked only for environmental, social and anti-war causes. It still exists today in San Francisco - the Public Media Center.

THEN, IN THE early 1970s, the first statistics on the advance of global television viewing were published. The average person in industrial countries was already watching about four hours of TV per day, and in some countries - notably the US - seeing more than 23,000 commercials per year. People were spending more time watching television than doing anything else in life besides sleeping, working or going to school. For a majority of people, television viewing was the main activity of their day: passively ingesting powerful imagery projected by a small number of commercial interests with intent. Electronic media were replacing direct experience of a wider world, substituting secondary and tertiary processed knowledge and experience; mediated reality; virtual reality. The Orwellian vision of mind control was near realisation.

What was true for industrial countries in the 1970s was soon true everywhere - people in grass houses in Borneo or in northern tundras were staring at satellite images of Dallas or Baywatch. Global mass media were morphing diverse cultural consciousnesses into clones of the commodity culture that dominated imagery, knowledge and experience. We see the outcomes nearly everywhere, today.

That was the point when I decided to write Four Arguments for the Elimination of Television, to amplify the invasive, controlling, stupefying, globally homogenising impacts of television, now in the hands of ever fewer global corporate giants.

At first, I never thought of Four Arguments as an anti-globalisation book. But now I do: the first of three books that are reiterations of similar warnings, via different prisms. The next book, In the Absence of the Sacred, covered two other related points: first, the role of other

19

modern technologies in alienating human experience, while ravaging the Earth; and second, the unique rapidly growing role of the world's remaining 300 million indigenous people in *resisting* that process.

INDIGENOUS KNOWLEDGE AND cultural, economic and spiritual practices are expressions of *non-mediated* societies rooted in direct contact with nature, operating from values nearly opposite to our own. They offer an antidote to the modern dilemma. It is no small irony, however, that the very success of indigenous peoples of the world in sustaining viable traditional societies over millennia, without destroying their lands or biodiversity - wildlife, forests, waters, biota - has also made them prime targets for modern resource-addicted global corporations who seek to invade and exploit those lands. Organised Indigenous resistance to these advances is now expanding on every continent, most spectacularly in South America in such places as Bolivia, Ecuador and Peru. These movements must be supported by non-indigenous activists everywhere.

In the *Absence of the Sacred* was published in 1991. In that same year, I began conversations that were arguably as significant for me as those with Brower, this time with Doug Tompkins, a friend of thirty years who had founded the clothing company ESPRIT. Tompkins told me he was quitting business, and asked me to help launch his new Foundation for Deep Ecology.

One of the first activities we agreed to work on was the grave threat of economic globalisation. If mass media represented the *internal* mental homogenisation process, then economic globalisation - the new global structures that transfer real power away from local communities and nation-states to global corporate institutions - represents the *external* unification, centralisation and homogenisation process; the remaking of economic and political forms to better fit narrow corporate purposes, with horrendous implications for nature. In 1993, we convened a meeting of leading thinkers and activists who were already at work on this problem - notably Edward Goldsmith, Vandana Shiva, Maude Barlow, Helena Norberg-Hodge, Martin Khor, Tony Clarke, Dave Korten, Walden Bello and Lori Wallach, among others. That, in turn, soon led to the formation of the International Forum on Globalization (IFG), and ramped up efforts to stimulate, through public teach-ins, publications and activism, an effective global opposition movement, which later burst onto the scene in Seattle. It also led me to partner with Edward Goldsmith for the third leg of the trilogy, *The Case Against the Global Economy, and For a Turn Toward the Local.*

OF COURSE ALL of this work continues today, with the increased focus of many groups on actualising viable alternative, local, ecological economics. And IFG has a new book, *Paradigm Wars: Indigenous Peoples' Resistance to Economic Globalization,* which surveys and supports that movement. To say that it all began with martinis with David Brower in New York may be stretching the point, but in my own life it certainly created the initial earthquake of consciousness that pushed me down many pathways to here.

Jerry Mander is the Founder and past President of the International Forum on Globalization and is now Senior Fellow. In the 1970s he formed the country's first non-profit advertising agency, Public Media Center, which campaigned internationally for Sierra Club, Friends of the Earth, Greenpeace and other environmental and anti-war efforts. He is also Program Director of the Foundation for Deep Ecology.

BIOLUXURIANCE

Most weeks I go to watch our local barn owl.

WHEN I WAS a boy, it was my lair, my emotional rehearsal room, my laboratory, my whole domain. Nothing special; just a Chiltern coombe, a scatter of small woods, a lost stream which mysteriously reappeared every seventh winter. But it was where I began to find my worldly bearings. I saw the red rumps of redstarts through my first pair of binoculars, glowing like hot coals. I buried messages for my first girlfriend under a great oak, and grubbed up the altimeter of a crashed bomber in a primrose copse.

I sat like some teenage Arthur on the slopes, swooning to Vaughan Williams on a portable radio. In some deeply atavistic way, I took possession of that valley, made it my niche. Its own bounds - the soaring hilltop beeches (called Heathen Grove!), that capricious winterbourne, the ancient echoes, the great seasonal flow of birds along the hedgerows I dogged myself - became my bounds too.

Then I cheated on it. I went away. I sold its great animistic whole-ness for a mess of details. When I came back (the year *Resurgence* was started) I found it had been chosen for the route of a four-lane trunk road. It was no longer a place I haunted, but it was still lodged in me like a lodestone. I began to fight for it, but didn't know whether I was pleading for my lost domain, or pursuing the public good. I spoke out for the scarce flowers that bloomed among the beeches and chalk-scrub, but not for my bursting young heart, out there on the hillside to welcome the first cuckoo. The sub-editors of one of the pieces I wrote for the local paper were bolder: "Doomed", they titled it, "The Lost Valley where the Wild Orchids Bloom".

Years later, I spoke out against the road in a public enquiry, and mentioned the colonies of wood anemones that flecked the green lanes in the path of the proposed road. It was a bad mistake, a hostage to fortune. The counsel for the highways authority beamed in gratitude. Wasn't it true that I owned a wood nearby, and hadn't I written very publicly about its wood anemones, and how prolific they were? How could the laneside flowers be of any value when the species was, by my own account, so common locally? I *owned* wood anemones, he seemed to imply. They must be enough. Enough not just for me, but for the whole community.

He was not being especially devious. He was using the same argument that had come to be the norm in nature conservation: the survival of species counted, scientifically important or "representa-tive" sites counted, but not individual organisms or the feelings of ordinary people towards them.

With hindsight that exchange seems like a metaphor. The posses-sion of nature, its apportionment to the human estate, have been the central questions I've worried over in more than thirty years of writ-ing. And when I was invited by the then Nature Conservancy Council

(NCC) to write a personal account of nature conservation in Britain, it was the theme that dominated the resulting book, *The Common Ground*. Working with NCC scientists was a revelation, a barefoot education in ecology. I learned about the provenance of ancient woodland, about the fragility of the thin skein of life on peat bogs, about endangerment and 'non-recreatibility'.

BUT I WAS BOTHERED about the narrowness of the NCC's remit. "Scientific importance" (whatever that means - what is scientifically 'unimportant'?) was fair enough, but what about social importance, cultural importance? Bringing rare species back from the brink was a crucial part of saving the whole intricate fabric of ecosystems. But shouldn't we also have been striving to maintain the common species, the backbone of natural systems, to keep cowslips part of everybody's experience, to ensure that the song of the cuckoo never become a myth, a folk-memory mummified on disc? And what did the 'streaming' of habitats, the notion of Sites of Special Scientific Interest, say about natural places that were not on the list? That they were uninteresting, valueless, someone else's responsibility? There were no such things as Sites of Special Aesthetic or Emotional Importance. Tough luck if your village copse was one of those, for you.

So *The Common Ground* argued for the importance of the common, and the commonplace, for the centrality of nature in the experience of all humans, not just scientists. Long before the term 'biodiversity' had been invented, it made an implicit plea for 'bioluxuriance', for a widespread richness of nature, both for the sake of humans and for wild organisms themselves. It was a perspective that eventually began to be given consideration by government and planning bodies. In my working life it led, in the 1990s, to *Flora Britannica*, that botanical Domesday Book, produced by tens of thousands of ordinary British people, about the role of wild plants in their lives. And it led to my buying a small wood in 1981, and attempting to put some of these ideas about the connections between nature and human communities into practice.

HARDINGS WOOD WAS, I think, the first privately owned 'community wood' in Britain, and we had to invent our practice and principles on the hoof. But I'm gratified that a style of wood-life we adopted chiefly out of ignorance and necessity and an uncomfortableness with management structures turned into something that, in retrospect, had a truly ecological shape. We had no fixed management plan, but practised a kind of on-site democracy. We tried (and again naivety and timidity played a part) to echo rather than smother natural processes, and our primitive burrowings and thinnings and trackmakings had more in common with the business of beavers and badgers than foresters.

And, most happily, the diversity of wildlife which resulted was reflected in a huge variety of human activity in what had previously been a dark and empty wood. I treasure the memory of one occasion when these efflorescences of different kinds of life came together: a very serious band of young children about the absurd but touching task of escorting frogs returning to their spawning pond.

Yet it was not simply the cultural flowering of the wood that left its mark on me, but the wild, self-willed quality of its evolution. The natural regeneration swamped our pointless attempts at planting. Supposedly sensitive plant species migrated round the wood in ways beyond any accounting. All the marks we made were mollified, absorbed, un-tidied up, in the wood's own development plan. It was a powerful lesson, and I now increasingly believe that we need to respect and learn from the anciently evolved wisdom of natural systems, not presume to manage or steward them according to our own principles.

For me, this is partly an ethical choice: all species (ours included) are of equal value. But it is also a practical matter. Our notions of the 'usefulness' of nature - that is usefulness to us - are not only selfish but ignorant. We have scarcely begun to understand the intricacy and reciprocity of the biosphere. It is nameless plankton in the oceans and unglamorous fungi in the soil - none of them the subjects of Green Revolutions or television documentaries - that keep the planet going.

Ironically, this realisation has helped me towards a personal reconciliation with science, a need to know more about other kinds of life on their own terms, not simply as creatures of my imagination. Most weeks now I go to watch our local barn owl, the first I have lived closely with since those childhood days in the valley of the orchids. It is, in the truest sense, a neighbour, and I cannot - as I have done in the past - reduce it to a symbol, make it my emotional puppet. I need to understand how it's getting on here, where it likes to be, what drives its odd reactions to the weather. Already I am learning to glimpse it as other birds might, as a fluctuation of light behind a hedge, as its teetering wings move like divining rods over the grass. But there is much more to do. To bridge that divide between the knowledge of nature as a collection of other beings in their own right and the fierce, luminous presence they have in our imaginations seems to me our next great task.

Richard Mabey is a writer and broadcaster with a special interest in the relations between nature and culture. His books include his award-winning biography of Gilbert White, and his recent memoir Nature Cure, which was shortlisted for both the Whitbread and Ondaatje prizes. He is Vice-President of the Open Spaces Society and lives in Norfolk.

BEYOND PEAK OIL

It seems to me that there is a simple formula to avoid economic collapse: start to reduce oil consumption now - by 3% per year.

Y PERSONAL INTELLECTUAL and spiritual journey began in the 1970s, and stemmed from an intense desire to understand why humanity is so obviously undermining the ecological basis of its own survival and that of countless other species. I also felt a profound need to explore alternative ways of living that, if adopted widely, might enable humankind to avert environmental catastrophe.

This journey took me to the realms of mythology, anthropology and indigenous wisdom. In some of my early books I sought to trace the origins of humanity's antipathy toward the rest of the living world to some ancient shift in consciousness coincident with the adoption of agriculture and the building of the first civilisations.

However useful this perspective may be in understanding how we got here, I eventually found it to be insufficient. Clearly, while modern patterns of exploitation and domination have ancient roots, matters have taken a dramatic turn just in the past two centuries. The human population has grown sevenfold; per capita rates of resource consumption have skyrocketed; and levels of economic inequality have also soared to new heights. Meanwhile, the impact of human activities on the natural world has also attained unprecedented levels.

What has changed? The decisive factor, it seems, has been our discovery and increasing use of fossil fuels - abundant, cheap sources of concentrated energy that have enabled us to expand our power over nature to a degree that would otherwise have been impossible.

Of course, our reliance on fossil fuels has come at a cost of pollution and climate change. But just as insidious is the fact of our utter dependence on energy resources that are limited in quantity and that are depleting within historically narrow time-frames.

Thus, during the past five years I have become immersed in the subject of peak oil, travelling widely to speak to audiences about the perils of a lifestyle of oil addiction and of the coming impacts of petroleum depletion. Cheap oil has fuelled economic growth through expanded transportation, industrial agriculture, and ever-diversifying plastics and chemicals industries.

Now, as petroleum enters its inevitable decline, we must find ways to adjust - not just by identifying alternative fuels, but by curtailing many of the activities enabled by this remarkable substance. It will be a daunting challenge, to put it mildly.

Modern societies have faced other challenges in the relatively recent past, including two world wars and a Great Depression. Human beings are remarkably adaptable. However, in the present instance the needed adaptation could be profoundly hindered by two likely impacts of peak oil - one economic and the other geopolitical.

28

A protracted and growing global scarcity of the world's most important strategic resource is likely to lead to a meltdown of economies, making needed investments in alternative energy technologies and new post-petroleum infrastructure more difficult. At the same time, competition between major world powers over remaining oil supplies is likely to increase dramatically, and could escalate into open conflict. This turn of events would have horrific consequences for human beings and the natural world; it would also overwhelm the ability of any society to accomplish the energy transition in a co-ordinated and peaceful manner.

Clearly, humanity needs a way to keep these economic and political perils at bay while addressing the complex problem of reorganising its industrial, agricultural and transportation infrastructure to function without oil.

IN 2002 I became aware that Colin Campbell, the British petroleum geologist who founded the Association for the Study of Peak Oil, had authored a Protocol to address this very situation. At once I realised that the Oil Depletion Protocol is practicable, that it would confer immense benefits to signatory nations, and that for the world as a whole it could make the difference between adaptation and survival on one hand, and chaos and disintegration on the other. It also became instantly clear to me that if I - who was devoting myself full time to talking and writing about peak oil - was having trouble understanding the Protocol's implications, then surely much effort would be needed to convey its meaning to the busy policy-makers who would have to ratify it.

The Protocol itself is so simple that its essence can be stated in a single sentence: Signatory nations would agree to reduce their oil consumption gradually and uniformly according to a simple formula that works out to being a little less than 3% per year.

My current work revolves primarily around publicising the Protocol: I have written a book on the subject, *The Oil Depletion Protocol: A Plan to Avert Oil Wars, Terrorism, and Economic Collapse*, and am working with the Post Carbon Institute to establish an Oil Depletion Protocol Project with a small staff, whose purpose will be to promote through education and activism the adoption of the agreement worldwide.

One of the promising strategies towards this end consists of inspiring and co-ordinating individuals and local groups to abide by the Protocol proactively, reducing their oil consumption by 3% per year - and to do so publicly and vocally, to prod policy-makers.

WHILE MY WORK with the Oil Depletion Protocol might seem to be a narrow response to only one of humankind's many problems, I view it as the emblem and essence of the efforts that will be necessary to our collective survival. Oil depletion is the modern face of the universal ecological dilemma of population pressure, resource depletion and habitat destruction. In the end, there are only two possible responses: self-limitation, or a culling of the population by famine, pestilence and war. Fossil fuels have raised the stakes of the ecological dilemma to new heights, and peak oil thus looms as a pivotal historic choice for humankind. The Oil Depletion Protocol represents the path of co-operative self-limitation, and may be our last, best opportunity to avoid nature's solution to human over- exuberance.

Richard Heinberg is author of seven books, including The Party's Over: Oil, War and the Fate of Industrial Societies *and* The Oil Depletion Protocol: A Plan to Avert Oil Wars, Terrorism, and Economic Collapse. *Richard is a Core Faculty member of New College of California. For more information on the Oil Depletion Protocol see* <www.oildepletionprotocol.org>.

THE ECO-JOURNALIST
DAVID NICHOLSON-LORD

THE GREAT URBAN INDOORS

Not drowning - not even swimming - but
waving goodbye to nature.

WHAT I'M ABOUT to write is a kind of parable. As befits a
piece which is partly retrospective, it's about the contrasts between
past and future. In particular, it's about a small part of the unfolding
future which I've glimpsed recently.

Not far from where I live, in south London, is a park with, backing onto it, some large and expensive houses. Since the houses are
priced towards £2 million, they're occupied by the new feudal plu-
tocracy of City and plc, and at the bottom of their gardens, where
the hoi polloi can rubberneck through the high wire fencing, a strange
little rash of new buildings has sprouted. There are at least three of
them now, as neighbour has copied neighbour; they look a little like
posh garden sheds and they cost upwards of £10,000. Unless you
knew the people concerned or had minutely observed the construc-

tion process, you couldn't begin to imagine what was going on inside them.

Each shed contains, not the old-fashioned implements of toil, but a small and perfectly formed swimming pool where, in peace and total privacy, the new plutocrats can pit their wills and their stamina against an electrically generated current precisely calibrated to their selected swimming speed. The pools are not much bigger than a bath so you can't swim anywhere even if you wanted to. You swim, and swim, but you stay in the same place. The technical term for this exercise is 'resistance swimming'. One of the models is known as an "endless pool".

IF YOU DATE the beginning of the environmental movement from 1962, the year Rachel Carson's *Silent Spring* was published, then *Resurgence*, born in 1966, was one of its very first progeny. I was at school then so am a bit older than the magazine, but when I compare the magazine's infancy, and my own youth, with our shared middle age forty years on, there are some striking contrasts.

My youth, or at least that part of it spent at home before university, was relatively impecunious, pretty much alcohol-free, fairly 'primitive' - open fires, no central heating - and almost totally carless: I walked, cycled, caught trains and buses. And although it wasn't rural - I was brought up on the outskirts of Manchester - there was a lot of nature about. We had an overgrown garden where I spent long periods up trees, a couple of nearby ponds, a wood and a semi-functioning farm within a few hundred metres and, beyond them, a peri-urban river valley with marshy bits and bulrushes. As for garden sheds, we had an outbuilding we called a toolshed. It contained, as it name implies, tools - rakes, hoes, spades.

Absolute wealth in those days was much less and inequalities less pronounced: ostentatious affluence seemed rare. No-one worried too much about crime, no doubt in part because there was less to pinch, and children routinely undertook long solo journeys on public transport without the protection of mobile phones. Children also contributed to household tasks - one of my jobs was to clean the grates and make the fires - and were regularly subject to tellings-off by 'strangers' in public when they misbehaved.

I imagine these sorts of recollection will be shared by most people of a certain age. Those who feel excluded from them - usually because they are too young to have any comparable memories of their own - often resort to satire. Yet one of the inevitable consequences of ageing - *any* ageing, even from one's twenties onwards - is that we acquire perspectives that are simply unavailable earlier. We neglect these perspectives, I think, at our peril.

I have no idea whether 'life' was 'better' or 'worse' in the 1960s: the question, as soon as you pose it, slithers out of control. What evidence we have suggests we're nearly three times richer, in money terms, but somewhat less contented. But when one looks at how attitudes to the environment have developed, it's difficult not to reach bleaker conclusions.

The orthodoxy is that environment has been mainstreamed, embodied in institutions, policies and attitudes, and that green civil society has never had it so good. It's a superficially attractive argument but it ignores some powerful countervailing forces. Among these I would list the rise of competitive individualism as the dominant planetary ideology; the primacy of 'feel-good' commercial values; the decay of belief in collective action, coupled with a growing fear of the public realm; and the spread of material wealth. In particular, that threefold increase in income has enabled people to gratify their appetites in ways undreamt of in the 1960s, turning wants into needs, moderation to excess, abundance to satiety. Alcohol and cars, both absent in my childhood, have become toxic. Children, taught to regard designer labels as a birthright, are insulted if you ask them to wash up. Possessions, now ubiquitous, are the feedstock of crime.

Our new wealth, far from strengthening planetary awareness, seems to have dissolved or at least diluted it. I'm not sure which is the more depressing - the relative absence of environmental concern among teenagers and twenty-somethings, the relapse of our attitudes towards other species, or the repeatedly demonstrated tendency of behaviour to change only when crisis is imminent. Thus, while the 1960s gave us environmentalism (and *Resurgence*), the 21st century, so far, has given us denial. In some all-encompassing way, human society has turned in upon itself and, partly as a corollary, our psychological freedoms - our sense of what it is to be a free individual - are trammelled and diminished. This, for me, is the most worrying change of all and I think it can be partly traced to the physical and demographic contexts of our lives.

OVER THE LAST forty years, the UK, and the world in general, have become more populous, more urban, more managed, trodden, dwelt on. In the UK there are some seven million more people - a city the size of London - than when *Resurgence* was founded, so that we live increasingly hugger-mugger with each other, our appetites and impacts much greater, our lives and living spaces, of necessity, more tightly controlled. For me, the ramshackle woods and ponds of the urban fringe have been replaced by the managed green spaces of suburbia. It's hard for kids now to find trees to climb in even if they were allowed to, gardens are getting smaller, tools are for the vanishing manual classes, and most professional lives are spent staring at a computer. As a species, we have moved into the Great Urban Indoors, with its manifold diversions and distractions, and we are simply losing sight of nature, except as an occasional occurrence at weekend or on holiday, and then usually in surrogate or replica form. Is it, therefore, any wonder that what we don't see, we don't think about much, or don't care for? Or that we withdraw into ourselves, our homes, our families, fetishising what they contain - décor, careers, possessions, progeny?

In that sense, the endless pool is a version of the future - a vision of where wealth, overpopulation, individualism and commercialism are taking us. It's about denial, certainly, but denial given a perverse twist by indulgence and extravagance - in this case, the pumping out of CO_2 emissions for an activity, like patio heating or power showering, that is essentially marginal. It's about how pathogenic our urban habitat has become - sedentary, claustrophobic, self-reflective - and thus about the contemporary ego, its obsession with body image, its deepening narcissism. It's also about our relationship with the world beyond home, office and city, or such of it as remains. When I saw the first endless pool being erected, it struck me as another of the over-ripe fruits of privilege, another sign of how the superfluously rich are shutting themselves away from the rest of us, but I now think that's only half the story. In reality it's a journey into onanism, solipsism and decadence - a solitary traveller in an ersatz environment, moving constantly, seeing nothing, going nowhere.

David Nicholson-Lord is an environmental writer, formerly with The Times, The Independent and The Independent on Sunday, where he was environment editor. He is chair of the Urban Wildlife Network, deputy chair of nef (new economics foundation) and research associate for the Optimum Population Trust. His books include The Greening of the Cities (Routledge, 1987) and Green Cities - And Why We Need Them (NEF, 2003).

PROPHETIC POLITICIAN
MICHAEL MEACHER

WHITHER THE ENVIRONMENTAL MOVEMENT?

I believe we cannot rest on our laurels when there is so much yet to be done.

WE SHOULD NOT get dewy-eyed about the achievements of environmental activism. It remains but one player in a crowded market, and a rather feeble and marginalised one at that, easily pushed aside when the going gets tough. Its leverage is weak - vision rather than muscle - and it is tolerated rather than embraced. But its time is definitely coming.

When I was elected to Parliament in 1970, the first environmental shoots were beginning to appear with the Stockholm Conference of 1972 on sustainability, and the Club of Rome warnings about the limits to world industrialisation. But the decade was dominated by the international turbulence unleashed by the quadrupling of the oil price, with the ensuing worldwide inflation paving the way for the Reagan-Thatcher monetarist kickback in the 1980s. The long war of attrition with the trade unions, the launching of untrammelled market liberalisation, and the rekindling of the 'special relationship' with the US then took precedence over all other concerns.

But the gradual recovery of stability and prosperity in the 1980s allowed the first glimmers of concern over environmental externalities: recognition of the damage done to Scandinavian lakes by acid rain and then the Thatcher speech on the dangers of climate change. But economic recession in 1990-3 rapidly brought the shutters down again. The political requirement for environmental progress - a favourable economic context - had been temporarily lost.

The long period of steady growth from 1993, however, opened up new possibilities. Concerns about climate change, pollution, genetic modification (GM), and the environment as an index of the quality of life, were clearly growing and their salience on the political agenda was rising. In my book *Diffusing Power* I emphasised the finite limits to material growth, the risk of global climatic destabilisation, and the pollution brought by so-called prosperity. The political response, however, was at best desultory. Neither Margaret Thatcher nor John Major was noticeably interested in the environment, and the general feeling was shallow rather than committed.

The watershed of 1997 offered hope of a new environmental era. As Minister for the Environment for the next six years I would certainly want to claim that advances, even breakthroughs, were made on several fronts and that the environment moved strongly up the political agenda - as the dismay of some of my colleagues would testify! Nevertheless I would also be the first to insist that the real political breakthrough was not made. The major industrial vested interests - nuclear, chemicals, food and drink, air travel, cars, oil and gas, agriculture - used their close links with Government ruthlessly to protect their own position. Tony Blair, like his predecessors, does not care deeply about the environment and will always give priority to Big Business, though he is more adept at appropriating the cachet that rhetoric about the environment brings.

In fact, as I gradually discovered to my chagrin, New Labour's view of the environment is not so much lukewarm as, at best, sceptical or, at worst, hostile. For the ideologues of the Blair Project, the environment is seen as anti-business when they want to be pro-business, regulatory when they support voluntarism, and anti-aspirational when they want wealth-creation and enrichment to be the dominant drivers. Regulation and taxing are out, while coaxing and incentives are the order of the day. What this means of course is that nothing will be done which significantly offends business - rather like saying the police must be persuasive and not do anything the burglars or muggers would seriously mind. That doesn't give a lot of leeway for environmental progress, as indeed we've all found out.

It's not of course formally presented like this. The spin is that sustainable development is the governing ideology, and social justice, economic efficiency and environmental protection are equally important and can all be optimised together. The same canard pervades the EU Lisbon Agenda. The reality, however, in an international capitalist economy is that economic performance and competitiveness overwhelmingly take precedence. Social and environmental justice are merely the greenwash to ward off charges of deepening social inequality and worsening environmental and atmospheric contamination. In practice, whatever the rhetoric, the second requirement for environmental progress - that ecological sustainability must not be allowed to be suffocated or swamped by the economic vested interests - has not been met.

This is not to say that progress has not been made at all. Of course it has. But it is far too little and perhaps too late. Climate change cannot seriously be countered if the Government (or Prime Minister) dithers about extending the Kyoto Protocol (to try vainly to win over George W. Bush), fails meaningfully to promote renewables (because government is still over-wedded to the fossil fuel industries), and builds new airports across the country and drops the fuel duty escalator on cars (because it panders to short-term consumerism over long-term environmental concerns). No Government can claim it is prioritising the environment when it resiles on its future commitment to renewables and energy conservation in favour of nuclear, when it obsessively pushes GM without testing the health and environmental consequences, and when it abruptly abandons long-prepared plans to require leading industrial companies to monitor and report on their environmental and social impacts.

NEED IT INEVITABLY be like this? I think not. A new energy and environmental world-order is coming; its outlines are already clearly visible - it is just sad that it is going to be forced on us rather than eagerly embraced by us as a visionary and inspiring goal for the whole of humankind. It is clear beyond any doubt that the current global regime cannot be sustained. The exponential increase in demand on the Earth's resources from the turbo-capitalism of unprecedented worldwide industrialisation is already leaving an ecological footprint that will require two Earths, not just one, by 2050. A global population that took Homo sapiens a million years to reach one billion has almost quadrupled within the last century to nearly seven billion. And climate change, most dangerous of all, could make large parts of the planet uninhabitable within this century.

By 2050 oil, the foundation of modern civilisation - the driver of industry, mechanised agriculture, transport and military capability - will largely have run out. Half or more of the world will be water-stressed. Fish stocks, a staple diet of a fifth of the world, already near-extinct in many regions, may have collapsed further. The impacts of climate change in destroying croplands, exacerbating water scarcity, and unleashing environmental refugees on an unprecedented scale - let alone generating runaway feedback effects from Amazon dieback, Antarctic and Greenland ice-melt, and deep-ocean methane hydrate escape - will change the face of our world irretrievably.

THE ROLE OF the environmental movement is to prepare the blueprint for a different and genuinely sustainable world-order and to mobilise the forces required to bring it into being. It needs not only what we know - carbon rationing, renewable energy, conservation of energy, contraction and convergence for greenhouse-gas emissions worldwide, demand management for an increasing range of resources, and stabilisation of populations, but other imperatives too that are only now coming dimly into view. But above all, as the props of the old order wither and collapse, the configuration of present-day power structures will inexorably break down too. The role of the political wing of the environmental movement is to harness the forces that will fill that vacuum.

Michael Meacher was Minister for the Environment in the Blair Government 1997-2003. Since 2003 he has been very active on a number of domestic and international issues, especially the background to the Iraq War and its consequences, genetically modified (GM) crops and climate change.

BUILDING A BETTER WORLD

"We shape our buildings; thereafter
they shape us." - Winston Churchill

IT IS ABOUT forty years since I graduated from the Bartlett School
of Architecture, University College London. This was the 'swinging
sixties' when architecture was emerging from the stringency of the
1950s and the Second World War with a new hope for a peaceful
Britain. A visit as a schoolchild to the Festival of Britain made a lasting impact on me with its brave new Dome of Discovery, Pylon and
Royal Festival Hall. Anything seemed possible in those heady days.

Much, if not most, of the emphasis was on following in the steps
of the pre-war international Modern Movement with its dominance
by such iconic figures as Le Corbusier, Walter Gropius and Mies van
der Rohe - less so, unfortunately on the 'organic' design of the
nature-loving Frank Lloyd Wright. There was a feeling around that
architecture could really build a better world. Grand designs for a

new infrastructure that harnessed the innovations of modern technology were all that was needed. High-rise blocks of flats with 'communal' open space to replace worn-out Victorian terrace houses, new multi-storey town centres to replace congested huddles of old streets, and even whole New Towns to give families from 'the smoke' another chance in new houses and jobs in the fresh country air.

It was against this brave-new-world background, and a couple of years in a big London architectural practice, that I applied for and was awarded a Harkness Fellowship for two years' further study and travel in the USA. I elected to study City and Regional Planning at the University of California, Berkeley. The course was highly theoretical and science-based with emphasis on computer models. But Berkeley itself, in the grip of anti-Vietnam-war protest and psychedelic dropping-out, was a real eye-opener, as were travels around America, seeing vast wilderness areas and Native American cultures, experiencing Lloyd Wright architecture first hand, meeting Lewis Mumford and visiting the string of little-known American New Towns such as Radburn and Greenbelt, and the newer Reston and Columbia.

Berkeley city-planner Melvin Webber had been invited over to advise on the master plan of Britain's biggest and most ambitious new city - Milton Keynes. His Los Angeles-style 'no-place realm' concept for a spread-out, low-density city gained favour and became the model. Central also was the concept of 'growth and change'. What was needed was a system to monitor and evaluate the city as it grew, to enable planners to respond quickly to its successes and failures and feed lessons into the next phase. This meant having clear objectives and targets to measure against. New City Corporation Chairman Lord Campbell was very keen on this and, freshly returned from Berkeley, it became my job to set up the system. But tensions developed between master planners and new Corporation departmental heads when early performance lagged behind the plan, and gradually the monitoring idea lost its shine.

A sabbatical in Los Angeles led to working with a vibrant Mexican-American community in a slum area. Back in the UK I soon opted for the gritty pace of city life and took on what was termed 'inner city stress areas' with a job as community architect for the Notting Hill Housing Trust (NHHT), a pioneering housing association in London. The success of NHHT lay in focusing on solving a family's housing problem within a small community area - often managing to re-house a family in a newly renovated flat only a few doors or streets away. The real leap forward came with the innovative concept of a Housing Action Area (HAA) where about 500 inner city stress area houses (many in multiple occupation) were designated to be brought up to minimum standards within five years. The local council and NHHT worked in partnership, and the Colville-Tavistock HAA became a pilot for others across the country, including those in the London Borough of Hammersmith and Fulham, where I next worked as community architect. Here, working from a small local office, we surveyed every single house and flat in the area, together with family housing details. A five-year action plan prioritised conditions and focused on the worst first. It was an ambitious plan and it worked. There was nothing like seeing the ecstatic faces of a local family who had just been shown their bright new flat. They just couldn't believe it after living so long in a damp, poky basement harassed by a grasping landlord.

COMMUNITY ARCHITECTURE IS one of the best ways to produce what local people really want. But in the early 1980s new environmental ideas beckoned and I decided to step into a new world. My wife Joss had started a new publishing company called Gaia Books and it was taking off. The concept of Gaia - the living planet - and the work of James Lovelock were completely new to me and captivated me straight away. Soon after I joined the company, we were on holiday walking the coast path around St Davids, Wales. "Why don't we combine my experience of housing design with the new ideas about Gaia?" I suggested to Joss. And so we did, and *The Natural House Book* was born, became a best seller, and led me to play a key role in the exciting field of eco-design.

The book took about a year to research and a year to write. During this time I had made contact with some special people doing exceptional things in 'green' design. It seemed a pity to lose contact with them once the book was done. So one evening in 1989 ten of us met at Gaia Books' offices in London and founded the Ecological Design Association (EDA). This was a network of architects, designers, artists and craftspeople who subscribed to the concept of ecological design. It is a marvellous thing to be involved in such an enterprise where struggling individuals suddenly realise there are others like themselves who share their beliefs and experience. This venting of pent-up energy was formidable and everything was possible.

We held meetings, conferences, exhibitions and produced a regular newsletter and a magazine, *EcoDesign*. Word got around and everyone wanted to join. At its peak we had around a thousand members and active branches around the country. The Annual EDA Lectures were launched and we asked the best eco-designers to speak - one of the most memorable being the late Victor Papanek. This new enthusiasm also led to the formation of Gaia International - an informal think tank of green and spiritual architects from Europe and elsewhere. By this time the reach of the Gaia movement was worldwide.

The EDA quickly reflected my earlier beliefs about what constitutes a natural house: ecology, health and spirit. The first was, and is, predominant and best known with its concerns for environment, sustainability and energy conservation. The second was less known and understood but potentially vital in a world where personal health was under attack from a world swamped with artificial chemicals and materials (and now also electro-magnetic fields and microwaves). The third was the Cinderella of the three, as spiritual values usually came bottom in modern design. But in reality this is the most important and should be the overall guiding light of any worthwhile sustainable design. For me, and from my experience over twenty years of eco-design around the world, finding a *balance* of the three is the key to good sustainable design and architecture.

My vision for the next forty years is of a benign architecture that is carbon-neutral, low-impact and uses sustainable materials and appropriate technology. It should be life- and health-enhancing and socially responsible, guided and empowered by local community and personal and spiritual values.

But there is another powerful influence that architects and eco-designers are not fully utilising at present. This is Nature - her cyclic processes of growth and decay, and her natural organic forms. Lloyd Wright and Bruce Goff and their followers saw this and produced some wonderful 'organic architecture'; so, too, have those inspired by Rudolf Steiner. But there is so much more to discover, and hopefully future architects and designers will look for their vision of the future to Nature and to Gaia for fundamental inspiration and truly sustainable solutions.

David Pearson qualified at the Bartlett School of Architecture in London and then studied in Berkeley, USA. He is author of nine books on natural architecture and design. He is a founder member of Gaia Media, Gaia International and the Ecological Design Association.

THE ACADEMIC ENTREPRENEUR
JEREMY LEGGETT

FROM CARBON TO SOLAR

Some flashbacks from the past forty years, and some dreams for the next forty.

1966 ENGLAND WIN THE World Cup. I watch agog in black and white, twelve years old, blissfully unaware that the world is completely dependent on a commodity over which nations routinely wage war, and that the global industry for which I will one day be a servant has already discovered the most oil in a year that it ever will. **1973** The first oil shock. I am at university, studying geology, learning how to find oil. A suave Saudi energy minister dominates the news bulletins as the price of oil climbs through the roof. Queues a mile long form at filling stations. Talk of economic disaster, and maybe even nuclear war. The Saudis, who produce the most oil, are angry with America, which consumes the most oil, about the Israel thing. The Saudi King has waved his oil weapon, a tap, which he can turn on or off at will. The world looks over the precipice.

Global oil supply falls only 9%, but a grim recession follows nonetheless.

1975 I graduate among the growing ranks of unemployed, and narrowly avoid working for Mobil. Instead, I go to Oxford to sweat my way to a Ph.D., researching the rocks of ancient oceans. My supervisor is W. Stuart McKerrow, an inspirational man. One of my mentors is Ron Oxburgh, future chairman of Shell, then a mere Oxford don. Men like these teach me to look at the big picture. In a world of narrow experts, they encourage me to take the multidisciplinary road.

1978 The Royal School of Mines at the Imperial College of Science and Technology is looking for a lecturer in Earth history. I apply, and get the job, against all expectation. I am twenty-four, a single parent, impoverished, cycling around Oxford with a happy daughter behind me in a child seat. I take the train to London each day now, and drink coffee with colleagues far older then me, many of whom have held high office in oil and mining companies. Like them, I begin an immensely lucrative sideline in consulting for the big energy companies.

The shah who rules Iran is deposed by an ayatollah. The oil price soars again. Iraq invades its neighbour, imagining it is weak, seeking to grab some more oil. The oil price tops $80 a barrel, in modern terms. The Second Oil Crisis is worse than the first, lasting into 1981.

1981 Now it is boom-time in oiltown. The industry has never made so much money. When were the most drill rigs ever? 1981. The most tankers? 1981. You get the picture. The industry has never since invested so much in trying to find more oil and get it to market.

The Saudis up the pump rate, new oil comes on the market from the North Slope of Alaska and the North Sea, and oil is released from stockpiles. Suddenly there is a glut. The price falls, and we enter a long period of low prices. It will last into the next century.

Mid-1980s I am researching the rocks of ancient seas and oceans, including oil source rocks, with funding from BP, Shell, and others. In the midst of another grim recession, I am wealthy now. Worrying papers start appearing in the scientific journals, written by atmospheric scientists warning about the future impact of greenhouse gases caused by the increasingly profligate fossil-fuel burning of recent decades. I read the results of the first climate models run on supercomputers. I know enough about the bottom part of the climate system - the oceans - to make the connections at once. The rates of global temperature rise estimated for a business-as-usual world will mean ecological and economic disaster.

1989 I quit. I can't stand the guilt of training servants for Big Oil and Coal any longer, let alone taking their petro-cash. I expect to be the first of a host leaving the fossil-fuel industries. I am to be sadly disappointed.

I JOIN GREENPEACE, and reprogramme myself as an environmental campaigner. From one of the most conservative universities in the world to one of the most radical environmental groups. Culture shock. I wind up working solely on climate, at and around the international climate negotiations. I become the acceptable face of Greenpeace, a scientist with a suit, mixing with the other scientists of the newly created Intergovernmental Panel on Climate Change (IPCC), squaring up to the growing legions of industry lobbyists at and around the negotiations.

1990 The first IPCC Scientific Assessment issues a stark warning which hits every front page in the UK. "Race to save our world," yells one of the headlines. Almost every government sends a minister to a World Climate Conference in Geneva that year.

1992 After three years of constant negotiations, I have seen things I can scarcely credit. Lobbyists from oil, coal, and a range of companies with mainstream energy interests doing everything they can to torpedo the negotiations. The carbon club, as I call them now, have obfuscated, distorted science, and openly orchestrated wrecking tactics by OPEC (Organization of the Petroleum Exporting Countries) governments. At the Rio Earth Summit, finally, a treaty is signed, but it has no teeth. The first Bush Administration, willing listeners to the men from Exxon, Mobil, Texaco, BP, Shell and the rest, have made sure of that.

1995 The Second IPCC Scientific Assessment. Worse news. Now the climate scientists think, by massive consensus, that the first footprint of human enhancement of the greenhouse effect has appeared in the sand. Renewed urgency at the negotiations. By now the carbon club's tactics are increasingly desperate. They are lying, demonstrably. At the 1995 climate summit in Berlin, governments agree that there will be a treaty with timetables for emissions reductions, and at the 1996 summit in Geneva they further agree that the targets must be significant, and legally binding.

1997 All eyes on the Kyoto climate summit. The carbon club's campaign plumbs new depths: television ads in the US saying that cutting emissions will wreck the world's number one economy. The reverse is true. Not acting: that's how to wreck the US economy, not to mention the global one.

BP finally breaks ranks, and quits the carbon club's main lobby group, the Global Climate Coalition. We have to act, CEO John Browne tells an audience at Stanford University. BP will be spending a bit more cash on solar energy to make the point.

The impact of BP's conversion is profound. Shell soon follows. Nobody can now claim that 'business' opposes a climate treaty. We want one, say BP and Shell. Bring it on.

I believe BP's sea change to be the single main reason that governments were able to negotiate the Kyoto Protocol. The Protocol calls for emissions reductions by industrialised countries summing to 8% by a window of 2008-12. It's a start. No more. Everyone knows that deep cuts are needed to stabilise greenhouse-gas concentrations in the atmosphere.

I LEAVE GREENPEACE and set up a renewable energy company, solarcentury. I no longer look to governments for leadership in solving the problem. Maybe some combination of business and consumers can provide leadership. I want to create a commercial microcosm of the kind of business that the world needs large numbers of. I choose solar photovoltaics. I don't view solar as a universal panacea; merely as an important member of a large family of low-carbon renewable and efficient energy technologies, all of which will have to grow explosively if we are to survive climate change.

1999 I move into the UK's first solar roof-tile home. I cut the carbon dioxide emissions from my home by over a tonne with a full refit of electricity-efficient appliances. The solar roof then generates more electricity than the home uses with constant occupancy, saving a further half-tonne. The average UK household produces six tonnes of carbon dioxide emissions a year. A 60% cut in greenhouse-gas emissions is the minimum needed to stabilise atmospheric concentrations, according to the IPCC. In round figures, that means a six-tonne home needs to cut by four tonnes, to two tonnes. The first two tonnes of the four are easily achieved with simple heat-saving measures. Add the one and a half tonnes I achieved with electricity savings and solar supply, and you are almost there. That's how easy it is. The government could change the building regulations to require this kind of action. More than half the nation's emissions come directly and indirectly from buildings.

2001 The newly elected US President, George Bush Junior, pulls the US out of the Kyoto Protocol. The rest of the world erupts in protest. At the Marrakech climate summit, outraged governments elect to go ahead with Kyoto without the US.

2003 The UK Energy White Paper sets a national target of 60% cuts in greenhouse-gas emissions, albeit not until 2050, and concludes that renewables and efficiency can make the necessary cuts to hit the target. Nuclear is put on hold for five years.

Spoiling a burst of optimism that he might now provide the missing leadership on climate, Prime Minister Tony Blair decides to join in with the US in its thinly disguised oil-grab in Iraq.

The hottest summer since records began descends on Europe, ruining crops, killing thousands. Finally, among the war-hero stories, global warming makes the headlines on a regular basis.

2004 We are becoming used to the Pentagon's smart bombs dropping on civilians, but then Shell drops a bombshell of its own. We are sorry, dear financial regulators, but we don't seem to have as much, er, oil as we said we have.

The biggest scandal in British corporate history unfolds. Why, I ask myself? I'd better check out what is going on. This is very important. The world is assuming it can run growing economies on growing supplies of generally cheap oil for several decades to come. If it can't, and supplies have peaked, all bets are off in the energy field.

The war in Iraq is not going well. Some rather unreasonable people are attacking the oil infrastructure, we hear. For this and other reasons, the oil price starts climbing. It crosses $40. Then $45.

My company is doing quite well. Blair visits it one sunny morning in September. He wants to give a speech in the afternoon announcing that the G8 Summit next year, which he chairs, will have global warming as one of its two main themes. Sniffer dogs and a dour chief superintendent from the anti-terrorism branch descend on our office, followed by the man himself, with the national media in tow. Several passionate young solarcenturians tell the prime minister, with cameras and tape recorders rolling, what they expect of their government when it comes to building solar markets so they can compete with the Germans and Japanese. Blair listens, and tells them it is important for government to lead. You know, convincingly.

2005 I HAVE FINISHED digging into the peak oil debate. The peak of production will happen this decade, I conclude. 98% probability level. I am writing a popular book about the problem and how it will conflate with global warming. The bad news is that I can't see how we escape an economic crash. The good news is that the tools needed for weaning society off its oil addiction can be the same as those needed for heading off the worst of the climate-change threat - provided panicking governments and companies don't pile back into coal, or try and melt twenty million barrels a day from tar sands, and the like.

The G8 Summit comes and goes, with Bush as intransigent as ever and Blair forgetful of his promises to the young solarcenturians. Deep in the summit statement is a significant passage, asking the Saudis to please be a little more transparent about exactly how much oil they really have.

That's July. Then in August the most likely person in the world to know the truth, Saudi Aramco's former head of exploration and production, comes out and tells *The New York Times* that Saudi Arabia will never pump twenty million barrels a day, as the world is expecting. Indeed, he says, it will find lifting output from ten-and-a-half to twelve difficult.

By now the mainstream financial institutions are becoming interested in peak oil. Nothwithstanding, peak oil has yet to make much of an impression on the traders who fix the oil price. But they have plenty of other worries to keep the price high, from Vladimir Putin's machinations in the East to Hugo Chavez's manœuvres in the West, via many another problem in between.

Then Hurricane Katrina hits New Orleans, shuts down much of the Gulf of Mexico's production, mashes a few refineries, and the oil price tops $70. Global warming is beginning to conflate with peak oil.

The bad news on climate is coming thick and fast now. Loss of Arctic ice is so serious that scientists are talking about a point of no return. The Gulf Stream is found to be slowing. Still the US tries to kill the Kyoto Protocol at the annual climate summit, in Montreal. They trigger such global outrage they are forced to retreat. The sorry game of slow negotiation will go on. Targets will be set beyond the 2008-12 Kyoto commitment period.

2006 Petroleum Intelligence Week sees records in Kuwait saying the country has only half the oil it officially claims. President Bush throws gasoline on the oil-price fire by admitting the obvious in his State of the Union address: that America is oil-addicted and has to kick the habit. More wobbles in the markets. The price jumps above $75.

Serious investor interest in solar and other renewables has grown steadily during the previous year. Now it soars. All of a sudden, the survival technologies are hot properties. My microcosm is one of them. We have turned ourselves into one of the fastest-growing UK companies. Our solar combined-heat-and-power roof wins best overall new product at Interbuild, the main trade show of the UK construction industry. Perhaps we can be a bit more than a microcosm? Whatever, there are now many companies like us. The future looks - how shall I put it? - interesting.

2046 CAN THE WORLD HAVE rebuilt its economies with survival technologies by then? Can the world be run on renewables and efficiency entirely, including transport? Yes and yes. Well before. These are disruptive technologies. They can explode into markets faster than most people imagine.

We will find out who is right about peak oil before the decade is out. For all those who hold the view that history is the key to destiny, the discontinuities will be seismic. Well before 2046, I predict, the world will be floating on a sea of solar and other cleantech energy technologies. Oil shocks, oil wars, and all the other dismal paraphernalia of the hydrocarbon age will seem so very... twentieth century.

Jeremy Leggett is chief executive of solarcentury, a director of the world's first private equity fund for renewable energy, Bank Sarasin's New Energies Invest AG, and a member of the UK Government's Renewables Advisory Board. His critically acclaimed account of the first ten years of global warming, The Carbon War, was published by Penguin in 1999.

THE SOCIAL TRANSFORMER
GEOFF MULGAN

THE ENEMY WITHIN

I am optimistic that we can change our world by
changing our hearts and minds.

THE STATISTICIANS TELL us that twice as many people are
politically active today as when *Resurgence* was founded. Many more
people are taking part in demonstrations, consumer boycotts and
campaigns than in the apparently rebellious 1960s, and many fewer
believe what they're told by people in authority.

There is much to celebrate in the waning of deference. Yet for all
the vigour of the activism we see around us, on issues as diverse as
debt and poverty, human rights and climate change, my sense is that
the politics of the 21st century will be a lot harder than the politics
of the last. The reason is that, perhaps for the first time ever, our enemies are no longer outside us. We're quite well-suited to battles with
foreign powers, evil corporations or heartless states. But now we face

many challenges where the enemy is us - our desires and our myopias may be what stand in the way of survival.

Like many people I've spent much of my adult life trying to reconcile an idea of activism, which is about changing the world outside, with an idea of enlightenment, which is about changing the world inside. As a teenager I was influenced by the dying embers of 1960s' and 1970s' counterculture, though I saw them as rather self-indulgent. Instead I became immersed in radical socialist organisations, which offered an alternative to the poverty, inequality and hypocrisy that I saw in the rich country where I was born.

Left-wing organisations are caricatured by their enemies as cold and soulless. Yet when I was a teenager I found an extraordinary warmth and vitality in the world's labour movements. They didn't just have good parties, and rich traditions of music, poetry and dance; there was also a truly internationalist spirit and a healthy scepticism. I also learned from them a worldview in which there is a solution to every problem - if only enough people are willing to sacrifice, to campaign, and to challenge.

THE SECOND FORCE that shaped me was Buddhism. When I was seventeen I spent a year travelling in South Asia. One day, I was wandering around a forest in Sri Lanka and I sat on the ground for a rest. I was greeted by an elderly fellow-walker dressed in a monk's habit, who started asking me questions: where was I from, what was I doing, what was I looking for? His name was Nyanaponika Thera. I later discovered that he was one of the sharpest thinkers of Theravada Buddhism. He encouraged me to stay in a monastery and study the Pali canon.

Over the succeeding weeks, we met for daily discussions, disentangling one of the oldest arguments: whether to change the world for the better we first need to change ourselves, or whether, as I had been taught by my political companions, life is too short and the problems too urgent so that politics had to come first. The arguments were inconclusive. But I never saw the world in the same simple light again. I was opened up to an ecological awareness of our connections to nature and life in its widest sense, and to the impermanence of so many of the things I valued.

Ever since, I have been trying to reconcile these two worldviews: the active and the reflective, the political and the spiritual. What holds them together is a belief that we can only live sanely by creating meaning even where there is none, and by acting as if life is a gift to be passed onto others. If we are privileged with power or money or knowledge we have to put it to work, otherwise it atrophies and ultimately corrupts us.

As an activist I therefore repeatedly looked for the places where limited energies could achieve most. I was fortunate that my first job was in the dying days of Ken Livingstone's Greater London Council (GLC) which was a radical, inspired and sometimes deranged administration, but far ahead of its time in pioneering equality, discrimination, fair trade and environmental issues.

When Margaret Thatcher abolished the GLC, I was lucky to spend time with the pioneers of the internet at the Massachusetts Institute of Technology. These technologists were true (if often very naive) revolutionaries: they were convinced that they held the future in their hands and that they would usher in an ultra-democratic world without hierarchies, governments or big corporations, and where the material waste of the industrial age would be ended for ever.

I then worked in parliament for a youngish MP called Gordon Brown; then I started up a thinktank, and finally I ended up in government, first as an adviser and then as a civil servant. There, rather to my surprise, I had the unusual experience of seeing lots of what I thought to be good ideas put into practice, and some fairly substantial improvements in the conditions of many groups, from homeless people to poor families.

THE ONE ADVANTAGE of this rather messy career is that I've learned quite a lot about how change happens - and how it doesn't. Although I value the details of good management and organisation, I've become increasingly convinced that Keynes was right when he said of ideas that the world is ruled by little else. Again and again I have seen ideas - from carbon trading and restorative justice to participative budgeting - pass through the three stages that Schopenhauer once identified as happening to many truths: "First", he wrote "it is ridiculed; second it is violently opposed; third it is accepted as self-evident." From this comes a cautious optimism that even the most intractable barriers can be overcome.

My optimism also comes from an unfashionable faith in politics. I don't share the disdain of politics that so many well-informed people have. There is a lot that's wrong with politics. Far too often it is captured by the rich and by big business, and far too often it is dishonest or short-termist. But much of what people dislike about politicians is really what they dislike about other people - their beliefs, interests and values which happen not to be the same as their own. Democracy, painful and messy though it is, is the only way for people to live together, and if we want others to give up their gasguzzling cars or their unsustainable lifestyles, in the end we have to persuade them.

Governments do have great power for good and ill. But much of the time they are as much followers as leaders, caught in the slipstream of what we sometimes call culture, or social change, the myriad of small choices that people make about how to live, or about what's important to them. That's why recently I have come full circle, from the centres of formal power to a small NGO in east London, which is now called the Young Foundation after its founder, Michael Young, who was one of the most remarkable people I ever met. He had something of a blind spot in relation to the environment (despite being a pupil of Dartington), but he was an unmatched alchemist of social change, and through his many creations (from the Open University and *Which?* magazine to DIY garages, and colleges where patients can teach doctors) he embodied an optimistic view of people's capacity to run their own lives. He knew that everything big has to start small, and he was never afraid to kick off new ventures on a shoestring.

His organisations were always about changing people's hearts and minds as well as institutions and structures. In that sense he was undoubtedly ahead of his time, attuned to the challenge of simultaneously changing ourselves and changing the world around us, and finding a better accommodation between the inner and the outer world. Many of his projects were about helping people to take responsibility for their lives and their situations, and wherever possible helping people to support each other. This combination of inner and outer change isn't important only for climate change and the environment. It's also how we will come to terms with much longer lives, or the growing incidence of chronic disease; or recasting education to fit it better to life.

THIS MAY BE the hardest thing humanity has ever had to do. If many of the enemies really are within us as well as outside we will need new methods and new languages that go beyond the traditional stances of anger and protest. We've known for a long time that a society of sheep must in time beget a government of wolves. Now we need to learn how to be neither sheep nor wolves but something entirely different.

Geoff Mulgan is director of the Young Foundation, a centre for social innovation. Between 1997 and 2004 he had various roles in the UK government, including head of the strategy unit and head of policy in the Prime Minister's office and before that he was the founder and director of Demos. His latest book is Good and Bad Power: The Ideals and Betrayals of Government, published by Penguin in 2006.

THE MORAL ECONOMIST
ANDREW SIMMS

RICHER? YES; HAPPIER? NO

I hope the Happy Planet Index will help solve the
ultimate economic problem: how to meet
everyone's needs, whilst living within
our environmental means.

T HIS YEAR SAW the loss of two giants of humane economics.
Both provided insight, common sense, and profound alternatives to
the conventional economic system over the course of *Resurgence* magazine's first four decades.

J. K. Galbraith, who passed judgement on the 1929 collapse of
the United States' reckless financial system and other fundamental
flaws of business-as-usual, died in Spring 2006. Only days before,
Jane Jacobs passed away. She spent her life understanding what made
local economies thrive or die and advocated clear-sighted solutions.

Most unusually for economists, both were brilliant communica-
tors. Galbraith was embraced and then rejected by the establishment

as the fashion in economic ideas changed. Jacobs was always the activist, campaigning and connecting at the community level. Between them, and whether or not people are aware of it, their analysis gave foundations to many of the positive solutions now offered to the malaise of economic globalisation.

Galbraith saw that a weakly regulated system in which the powerful are free to pursue their interests may be capable of accumulating wealth (as well as destroying it) but is very bad at distributing, or 'irrigating' it among the whole population. He also prefigured the growing field of research into the economics of wellbeing by observing as long ago as the 1950s that a society based primarily on maximising people's material consumption is not a happy society. Later in life Galbraith also saw the increasingly obvious clash between ever-rising economic growth, consumption and fuzzy environmental limits.

Jacobs, on the other hand, from her writing in the 1960s on the complex life of cities, implicitly understood that economies were like ecosystems. She thought diversity and highly specialised local adaptation created the most vibrant, productive and satisfying environments. To her, the urban planners' slash-and-burn approach to regeneration coupled to the march of the remotely owned modern chain store was anathema. They had the same impact on communities that chemical-intensive, industrialised agriculture was having on the land. The result was a lot of pain with only short-term and questionable gains. Real solutions, she wrote, grew out of thousands of tiny human interactions: "Sidewalk contacts are the small change from which a city's wealth of public life may grow."

Economics is routinely used to rationalise cruelty in the self-interested pursuit of gain by a powerful global minority. But this hides the fact that it was once, even in the hands of Adam Smith, the father of classical economics, supposed to be a 'moral philosophy'. In the past four decades economics has drifted ever further into mathematical abstractions that, due to frequently absurd assumptions about human motivation and the nature of the economy - such as assuming that both people and ecosystems are reducible to simple, yet abstract, monetary equations - are not only detached from the real world but ineffective, dangerous and, for many, fatal. This emerges in the inability of markets to respond to global challenges like climate change and in the corrosion and undermining of the public domain in areas such as health and education.

THIS LEAVES US with two choices. Either, as Keynes said, we should remove economists from their priest-like status among policy-makers, and see them more on a level with, say, dentists, or we need to restore the notion of a moral economy. The problem is, just say the word 'economics', and most people's eyes begin to glaze over. Bewildering graphs from half-forgotten school memories act like anaesthetic on the mind. We need to find a better way to talk about economics as if people and the planet mattered. We need metaphors that are both immediately memorable and meaningful, and speak of deeper processes that can be explored later in depth, as desired.

Here are some examples, a wildly incomplete list that may leave you inclined to go away and think of more of your own. What are some of the big things that have become much clearer in the last forty years that now influence, or should influence, our economic way of life? And how can we successfully argue for the resurgence of a moral economy?

The paradox of economic freedom
One of the biggest struggles is over the notion of freedom.

Freedom is a big issue in economics that raises many questions about what it means to be free, how freedom can flourish, what can destroy it, and freedom's paradoxes.

The economic globalisation of the last forty years marched beneath a flag of 'free markets'. And, who could be against freedom? By definition it liberates. Its appeal as an idea explains why a creeping international coalition of economic think tanks committed to extreme market economics groups itself under the banner of the 'economic freedom network', milking the idea's attraction. The network's website is called 'Free the World.com'. Sadly, the ideas they promote produce the very opposite of freedom. And, surprisingly, this is something even conservative thinkers have clearly pointed out.

In *The Open Society and its Enemies*, published in 1962 when neoliberal economics was beginning to mount its challenge for power, conservative philosopher Karl Popper observed that "Unqualified freedom … is not only self-destructive but bound to produce its opposite - for if all restraints were removed there would be nothing whatever to stop the strong enslaving the weak. So complete freedom would bring about the end of freedom, and therefore proponents of complete freedom are in actuality, whatever their intentions, enemies of freedom." He applied his insights specifically to the economic domain and, in the light of the huge growth of multinational corporate size and power since, their importance is even greater.

The logical conclusion of this fundamental insight lies at the heart of countless economic arguments. Just as we need to garden to prevent plants being suffocated by invasive weeds, so economies need checks and balances to prevent the abuse of power. Yet the thrust of most economic policy is towards a teenage fantasy of a rule-free global economic playground, forgetting that playgrounds without rules get brutalised by bullies.

After learning that advocates of extreme free market economics are, in an Orwellian fashion, actually 'enemies of freedom', what else have we got wrong? Here's a checklist:

People really aren't just motivated by money: A now-classic study compared the different approaches of health services in the UK and the US to blood donation. In the UK people give freely; in the US they are paid to do so. Conventional economics predicts that the financial incentive should leave the US better off. But the opposite happened. The financial element lowered people's intrinsic motivation to donate for the common good, attracting only people more desperate for cash. Because these were drawn from people with higher incidence of drug addiction and health problems the blood was poorer quality and the whole service was more expensive and less efficient.

Having more doesn't make you happy: In 1962, to support the whole world's population at UK levels of consumption would have needed all the world's available biocapacity. Today, with consumption levels much higher, we would need three planets like Earth. But for the last three decades we have become no happier. Happiness, the research tells us, once our basic material needs are met lies in the quality of our friendships and family life, and the opportunities we have to be creative.

We can't have our planet and eat it: Taking a typical calendar year, overall the world starts living beyond its environmental means on 23rd October. Where many individual rich countries are concerned, the date is much earlier - 16th April in the case of the UK. Yet, many millions globally still do not have their basic material needs met. We have to cut back on over-consumption to free up the environmental space to meet others' basic needs. Because we have eyes bigger than the planet, we need to measure the planet's environmental equivalent of its assets and cash flow, just as you would with a business to prevent it going broke. At the moment, governments don't even have a set of ecological accounts.

Economic growth isn't working: In the 1980s, to generate $1-worth of additional income for the world's poorest people, it took a total of $45 of economic growth. In other words, for the poorest to get one dollar-sized slice of the economic cake, you would need a cake of 45 slices. But today, things have got much worse. Their share has shrunk. Now, to deliver the same-sized single slice of poverty reduction, the economic cake would have to have 166 $1-sized slices. That means we are much less efficient at reducing poverty, as it now takes far more resources and much more economic growth to reduce poverty by the same amount compared to the 1980s.

Markets fail: Another irony of the last forty years is that the free market voices that railed against economies being run centrally by the state have merely created a world in which economies are centrally run by corporations. The result can be just as inefficient. Market failure means that biggest isn't best. In two recent examples some of the biggest, most 'successful' internet access providers were shown to give the worst service. And when telephone directory enquiries were deregulated, the company which quickly became the UK market leader also provided one of the worst services.

ECONOMICS AS A moral philosophy, not detached mathematics, can be put to the service of humanity. But only if it understands that the economy is a wholly owned subsidiary of the environment. As John Ruskin wrote, "there is no wealth but life". What, for example, might be a more useful focus for study in our search for a sustainable, just economy that promotes wellbeing rather than crude growth for its own sake? nef (the new economics foundation) is publishing something we call The Happy Planet Index. By combining data on the ecological footprints of countries with information on human wellbeing, it will show the ecological efficiency with which it is possible to have a good life. By understanding the best and worst ends of the scale, we may just solve the ultimate economic problem: how to meet everyone's needs whilst living within our environmental means. If Jacobs and Galbraith were still alive today, I believe that this would be the question uppermost in their minds.

Andrew Simms is the author of Ecological Debt: The Health of the Planet and the Wealth of Nations, and policy director of nef (the new economics foundation) <www.neweconomics.org>. He was one of the original and leading advocates of the Jubilee 2000 debt relief campaign. In his work on local economies he named the emerging phenomenon of Clone Town Britain.

THE BUSINESS MAVERICK
ANITA RODDICK

BUCKING THE SYSTEM

I don't just want corporations to be responsible
I want them to shift their energy into making the
world cleaner and fairer.

I DON'T THINK I had the slightest intention of going into business in 1966. I certainly never saw a copy of *Resurgence* that year. I
wanted to be a television director, a magnificent teacher, or an actor.
I was turned down for drama school, but teaching in the 1960s
could be hugely dramatic too. I dragged a group of kids who were
studying the history of the First World War to France. We hitched
there and slept in the trenches that still remained. We read Rupert
Brooke poems. We acted out Joan Littlewood's *Oh! What a Lovely War*. I
can't imagine any teacher being able to do that nowadays.

I went travelling, I opened a café in Littlehampton and I even
planned to start a pineapple plantation in Australia. It was the height
of the Vietnam War and I certainly saw myself as an activist. I was

involved in the local CND and Shelter groups. In fact, the invasion of Centre Point was planned in my kitchen. I don't think at that time I ever imagined that my activism would take the path it eventually did, but actually I was learning then many of the most important things I needed to know to make The Body Shop different.

Travelling in Africa and the islands of the Indian Ocean certainly taught me the crucial importance of story-telling - I have always regarded telling stories about the people behind your products as far more effective than marketing. It also locks companies into some kind of moral framework. If you can't tell stories because the people who make the things you sell are semi-slaves in anonymous sweatshops, you operate at a distinct disadvantage. So ten years later when I opened The Body Shop, I did have some idea about telling stories instead of advertising - and about the environment.

Hardly anyone could even spell the word 'environment' in 1976, but I think we sensed that the real wisdom-seekers of the planet were the environmental groups, and we listened, and still do - they give us direction and an opportunity too.

Still, I have to confess that some of it was luck. I chose refillable plastic bottles - originally designed for urine samples - because I couldn't afford very many of them. I chose dark green to cover up the stains on the wall.

The bookies down the road were laying bets that I would be out of business within six months. The funeral parlours on either side of the shop were sending me solicitors' letters saying our name was disrespectful to the coffins that passed by each day!

We were enthusiastically naive, but it saved us from taking ourselves too seriously as businesspeople. We just had this idea that we had to tell stories. The products were bizarre. They had bits floating about in them. We used to tell people there were black bits in the

69

honey cleanser because the bees didn't clean their feet when they went back into the hive.

Then women were coming to the shop saying: "I like this." I could fill the bottles in the back, and handwrite the white labels. It was like a cottage industry, but it was fun. We had this intimacy, which is so important to real business - and which I have struggled to retain in the company ever since - and it was not for five years or so that we suddenly realised we had stumbled on something unique. We created this market, even though we didn't actually know what marketing was.

THE TRUTH IS that I never meant to be a big boss. But somehow in those beginnings, we - that includes staff, customers and franchisees - created something that spread to 2,045 shops in around fifty countries. Quite what that something was, and how it could be nurtured, is something I've spent much of the past quarter-century working out. I never went to business school or read any economic textbooks on the subject. I believed business was about buying and selling, rather than some kind of arcane financial science.

But even if I had read them, and got my MBA, I don't think it would have helped. There was no rulebook about how to run an inclusive, ethical company that was based - above all - on excitement and creativity. The fact that there is now is largely down to what we did over the past quarter-century.

Yet my ignorance of management theory turned out to be vital. I didn't stick to the rules because I didn't know there were any, and our very difference was a major factor in our success. I didn't know *not* to run the company in an inclusive way, blurring the distinction between retailing and campaigning. I didn't know *not* to take the company to places - community trade or human rights - where our competitors would never follow.

Going public was a major mistake. It handed over the ultimate ownership of the company to speculators and analysts who had absolutely no inkling of what we were trying to do. In 1987, I made a speech at the CBI after we had been voted 'company of the year', and called these people "dinosaurs in pin-stripes". I looked up after I said it, and there was Robert Maxwell walking out in protest.

Since then, I think we proved that putting a child development centre into a workplace isn't necessarily an eccentric thing to do. And if you want creativity from your staff, trying to create something closer to joy in the workplace isn't actually flaky at all.

I think we demonstrated - when we took on Shell after the execution of Ken Saro-Wiwa - that companies can challenge each other over the ethics of how they behave. Just as we demonstrated that companies could show some emotions more complicated than just greed and fear - though unfortunately, precious few of them do.

Going public gave us the chance to invest in our huge manufacturing plant. But although the constraints of ownership on the stock exchange are not total, they are constant. You never have time to reflect and pause and say: "Are we having fun?" "Is work joyful?" "Do we want to grow this year?" "Why don't we just have more fun with our employees?" "Why don't we do more social activism?" So you never have that real freedom to be able to take the identity of your company - which is, in essence, your own identity - and form it into something else. You're structured by the profit-and-loss sheet.

Despite those constraints, we pioneered community trade links with impoverished communities around the planet, with partners like Teddy Exports in Tamil Nadu, South India. We first bought massage items from their woodworking shops back in 1987. Our purchasing meant that Teddy Exports could expand to employ fairly and ethically, almost 500 people.

Most of the predominantly female workers were previously unskilled agricultural labourers, employed on a casual basis with little security. They were paid a monthly salary for safe, stable work, with no discrimination on the basis of religion, caste or disability. Because of that community trade link, they were able to open a primary school for 200 pupils, with evening classes for children working in factories in the area. They were able to set up health workshops and a vet service. It made a difference there and in the other twenty-eight community trade partnerships we set up. Because of them, The Body Shop supports thousands of family farmers and women's co-operatives - the kind of small-scale economic initiatives that are a real, sustainable antidote to poverty.

MY MAIN DISAPPOINTMENT is how few other companies have followed us down that path - to make their central purpose the elimination of poverty. The main reason I am so excited about L'Oréal buying The Body Shop is that the terms of the sale commit them to rolling out community trade throughout their company. And since the announcement of the sale, a number of other big companies have asked for help to do the same themselves.

If this works, it marks a real shift, spreading fair trade, and direct links with poorer communities, throughout the business world. I was never over-excited about corporate responsibility: I don't just want corporates to be responsible - I want them to shift their energy into making the world cleaner and fairer. That is why I'm thrilled to be involved in this.

And, yes, it has been controversial. But then one of the paradoxes of trying to push forward the boundaries of business behaviour is that you face constant criticism from two groups of people.

One is the business dinosaurs - people for whom a brave, idiosyncratic, maverick fight for human rights or social justice in business is a threat to everything they stand for. The other is those people who regard you as a symbol of something, and who - even though they may be columnists for Murdoch newspapers - believe you are constantly in danger of 'selling out'.

The truth is that real change in business requires both insiders and outsiders. They may despise each other for their compromises or their idealism, but nothing happens unless they both work simultaneously for change. Both have been reflected in the pages of *Resurgence* over the past four decades. Both are making honourable contributions to change, and I hope that in that time I have been - and in the future I am going to be - both of them.

Anita Roddick died unexpectedly in September 2007. She was founder of The Body Shop and a tireless activist/campaigner on the issues of human rights and social and trade justice. <www.anitaroddick.com> <www.takeitpersonally.org>

CLOUD GURU
DEEPAK CHOPRA

DISPELLING THE DARKNESS

I knew everything about medicine and
almost nothing about healing.

IT'S BEAUTIFUL UP here, sitting on a plane staring at clouds. Or should I say, it's still beautiful? There are invisible dangers in the atmosphere. The toxic breath of industry, the careless debris of The Good Life being led down below. I know this, yet these white billows, rank upon rank, look so pure that for a moment one forgets.

Thirty-five years ago, on a long migration from India to America, I wasn't worried about the clouds getting dirty and poisoned. I wasn't worried about anything. That trip was all excitement and confidence. I had a new bride by my side and a job offer clutched in my hand. Every ambitious young man I knew back in Delhi was facing West, and when word got out that the Vietnam War had created a doctor shortage in the US, I couldn't wait to make the leap. I expected The Good Life to come my way, and it did. I expected The

Good Life to make me happy, but it didn't.

I put in almost twenty years of effort to prove both things to myself. Camped out in a threadbare New Jersey motel that first night, I switched on a colour television for the first time in my life and saw a bloody victim of gangland violence being rushed to the hospital. *Oh my God*, they were taking him to the emergency room I would be working in tomorrow. In a sense those few ingredients - patients in need, colour TVs, and rushing from one hospital to the next - became hallmarks of my new existence.

But by 1980 I felt adrift, seeing myself as someone who knew everything about medicine and almost nothing about healing. After casting about aimlessly, I did something none of my Indian friends were doing: I turned my face East again. Not just out of personal restlessness. Not just to find God, because that wasn't my intent. I kept thinking about something else: why does the pursuit of happiness make us so unhappy? I had devoted myself to finding happiness, yet a looming, warning figure stood in my way.

That figure was the guru. Westerners glamorise gurus into spiritual superstars or demonise them as arrant charlatans. But in India a guru is more like your conscience. Strictly speaking, the Sanskrit word *guru* means dispeller of darkness, but in everyday life gurus are like a nagging inner voice reminding you that there are higher things to live for. Needless to say, gurus don't equate with The Good Life.

We are guilty in India of using gurus as spiritual anodynes, harmless as an English vicar but good for the soul. I decided to take them seriously, because for centuries the gurus have painted a clear picture: there are two ways to live - one is the pursuit of pleasure, the other is the pursuit of *moksha*, or liberation. The two roads sharply diverge, which is why The Good Life and gurus don't mix. I had proved to myself that pleasure, in and of itself, leads to exhaustion

75

and inner deterioration. What could the guru offer instead?

I won't recap my years with Maharishi Mahesh Yogi, except to say that the impact of a guru was everything I had hoped for and more. I found inner discipline and silence, not as ends in themselves but as openings to a great, unknown subtle realm that permeates nature. Next, I came to trust in another face of the guru, known as *upaguru*, or the teacher who is close by. Upaguru can be anyone or anything, whatever experience brings a flash of insight, a small step toward liberation. I have sat in lonely hotel rooms in Paraguay or Dubai and idly turned on the television, only to have the next image on the screen bring a sudden epiphany.

ONCE YOU ARE committed to dispelling your own darkness, guru is everywhere. After thirty-five years on the path, this has proved the most valuable lesson. And now I believe it is the lesson humanity has to learn. Why is our planet on the verge of ecological catastrophe? Because everyone wants The Good Life. They want it in Khartoum as much as in midtown Manhattan. As long as The Good Life means sensual pleasure, the acquisition of cars, houses, planes, boats, vacations, jet skis, and so on, we are in peril.

Staring at the clouds today, I see guru. The message of the clouds is the same as the message of Vasishtha or Ramana Maharshi or any other true guru: *See yourself anew*. We will not save the planet so long as we see ourselves through old eyes. If humans are animals that insatiably crave pleasure, we are lost. But happiness can be defined by the other road, the pursuit of liberation. I will never be free as long as I am an isolated individual struggling against nature. Freedom comes from surrender, and the first surrender must be to nature itself.

Nature is a cloud. It has no boundaries. It is incredibly pure and beautiful. Its motions are unpredictable. Clouds are always here, yet they appear and disappear, seemingly at random, always in the service of life. To adopt such an existence for ourselves is possible. Humans have always been sky-watchers: we have identified with what lies beyond the clouds.

So the guru's choice remains as clear as ever. I don't imagine that anyone will buy prime time ad space to declare that upaguru is the way of the future. But revolutions crop up unexpectedly (like clouds, once again), and I believe the present ecological crisis has its inner dimension. The next revolution, the one that will save us, will arise inside. When it does, humanity will experience itself in a new way, and when our descendants gaze at the clouds, still beautiful and pure, they will murmur to themselves, "Ah, it's true. I am that."

Deepak Chopra is the founder of the Chopra Center for Well Being <www.chopra.com> and President of the Alliance for a New Humanity <www.anhglobal.org>

THE GREEN NETWORKER
PETER LANG

GREEN GENEROSITY

I believe that if we harnessed the spirit of
co-operation within the environmental movement,
our influence would be greater
than the sum of our parts.

A RELATIVE RECENTLY asked me for advice about a new business he was starting - a business with a green tinge to it. Hitherto he had not shown any particular interest in the environmental crisis we face and he was duly grateful when I suggested some people he might approach.

In particular he was surprised when I said most of these people would be unlikely to want payment for their help: they would talk to him because they supported the type of business he was starting. As a businessman this was not a response he was used to: in his world where work is done for profit only, asking for assistance is tantamount to agreeing to pay the resulting invoice.

In the non-profit sector, I explained, different criteria apply. I have worked in campaigning organisations, charities, a political party and development organisations for over twenty years and the aspect that has always sustained me has been the generosity of spirit I've found. Such generosity is not, of course, unique to the green movement, but there is something about caring for the planet rather than profit which brings out this generosity.

It is an aspect of humanity which flourishes in our green movement, and for many of us it is an aspect which helps keep us involved in the long term. This generosity feeds the soul and provides an extended family. But it is an element which is stamped out in the globalised economy where the bottom line of profit is the only criterion for deciding on a course of action.

IN THE ENVIRONMENTAL movement, my perception is that most people enjoy their work: they find it fulfilling and will often work hard to fulfil the organisation's goals which they wholeheartedly support. This is not to say that every non-profit organisation is successful in its aims and brings joy to its staff. Indeed, there are two ways the environmental movement could work more effectively, and do so by harnessing this generosity of spirit.

The first is that our environmental and social justice organisations should be co-operating more. Many sectors have liaison organisations - BOND for the development charities, the Transport Round Table for the transport groups, and Sustain for the food organisations. But how much do we *really* work together?

While in the last thirty years the environmental movement has won the argument about the *problems* we face, we have yet to have our *solutions* taken on board. Politicians and businesses respond to us partly by the strength of the arguments we put, and partly by the pressure we apply. The pressure is always measured against the effect on votes and the influence from other, often more powerful groups in business and industry. By harnessing our co-operation we should be able to match that pressure from society's more powerful groups. The UK has a vibrant non-profit sector, and most hold yearly strategic reviews of what issues they are to focus on, and who to pressurise. Most of them make these strategy decisions on their own.

But imagine the effect if the entire environmental movement co-operated closely on issues, each using its own way of working to create a collective pressure which might match or even surpass the influence of the corporations and their lobbyists.

Imagine a Monday morning when government and a particular industry find themselves deluged with letters from constituents demanding action on an issue - co-ordinated by Friends of the Earth. The company's head office sports a banner hung by Greenpeace activists. Representatives from ethical unit trusts call because they are considering selling the company's shares. The Environmental Law Foundation initiates a private prosecution against the company. Forum for the Future offers its consultancy services, which can advocate much bigger changes. *Ethical Consumer* reveals the company's more unattractive behaviour. *Which?* magazine advises against buying the company's products. Green Party MEPs ask that the European Commission take action. Constituents visit MPs' surgeries and ask that they sign an Early Day Motion on the issue. The Fair Trade movement announces that a new ethical company is to launch selling similar products. All on the same day!

The effect would be that our influence would be greater than the sum of our parts. We would harness that aspect of the environmental movement - generosity of spirit and commitment - which business and industry can never have because of the way they are set up.

THE SECOND WAY our environmental movement could increase its influence is by assisting those parts which aren't performing as effectively as they might. There is one very important area of the environmental and social justice movement that needs help from its brethren. It's the organisation that - if it were successful - would help the rest of the movement to surge ahead in leaps and bounds: the Green Party.

Britain is signed up to international treaties which influence what we can and cannot do: the EU and the World Trade Organization are two of the most significant. But ultimately how our country is run still rests with the government we elect. Our parliament may have many faults but it is the MPs who set the framework within which our environmental movement can have influence. The changes we need to make depend on how our MPs vote.

Environmental pressure groups guard their political independence tightly: they resolutely won't give more support to one political party than another. This despite the fact that there are great differences in the extent to which the different parties have policies which protect the environment and promote social justice.

The result of the environmental movement being supposedly 'non-political' is that its members protest *outside* our legislatures. Our campaigners adopt an issue; we shout outside our town halls and houses of parliament and hope that an understanding MP or councillor will take the issues on board.

Across mainland Europe, however, the picture is different. Green MPs sit in most levels of government in most of the UK's European neighbours. In the main they attract 10-15% of the vote. The result is that every environmental and social justice issue adopted by the pressure groups has built-in support *already inside the parliamentary chambers*. There are elected Green politicians more than prepared to ask awkward questions such as how consumption levels can continually expand on a finite planet.

But here in the UK the group that the environmental movement needs to be elected - the Green Party - faces odds that no other part of the movement faces. And despite the fact that the rest of our movement *needs* Greens to be elected, it gives the aspiring Green politicians hardly any help.

A more imaginative approach to our relationship with political parties is needed than the "We're not party political" standpoint. The non-party-political stance has been adopted in a political system with a democratic deficit. The recent new economics foundation report *Spoiled Ballot* concludes that in general elections, despite the principle of one person one vote, 30% of the population wields 70% of the democratic influence because of the effect of 'first past the post' elections and different constituency sizes.

It is time the environmental movement re-assessed its commitment to being non-party political. By not recognising the democratic deficit and the benefits of Green MPs - whether of the Green Party or others - we are not wielding the influence we need to solve the environmental crisis.

After forty years it's time the environmental movement recognised the strength of our culture of co-operation and generosity, and harnessed it to maximise our influence. It is a rare strength: we don't make enough of it.

Peter Lang is Resurgence's Events Director. He is the co-founder of Green & Away, which works with many environmental and social change organisations. He previously worked for the Green Deputy Mayor of London and the Green Group in the European Parliament.

IMAGINATION HOLDS THE KEY

I believe that this is no time for navel-gazing: it's a
time to actively create ideas and institutions
to work with the grain of nature.

SELF-KNOWLEDGE CAME to me in a hurtful wave. I was shallow. A thought of even fairly small draught would bottom out on the rocks of my ignorance. Oh, I wanted to be deep, but my body never felt right in a James Dean T-shirt: I was just too tubby and far too optimistic to do 'mean and moody'. It felt ridiculous. Nor could I do the haggard troubled soul philosopher bit. However, the saving grace is that I eventually came to the conclusion that to get by I had to come at the world with innocence and adopt the tactics to simplify what I saw and felt into bite-size chunks so that I could digest them easily.

This approach irritates a lot of people. Why? Because complexity is the veil behind which vested interest lies. "If people just observed common courtesy the only problem in the world would be personal health." Can you find a flaw in this sentiment? I can't.

People have far more in common than we feel comfortable in recognising. Our vanity makes us want to believe that we are fiercely individual and the marketing demands of a consumer society encourage this illusion. However, our basic material needs for shelter, food, warmth and health are common and I would suggest the need to feel needed, respected and loved fit that bill too. Our fears focus almost entirely on ensuring that we have all of the above.

When we do have most of those things in place, we start to muse about the meaning of life. The Big Question: why are we here? And its gloomy attendants: fear of death, and the profound hope that there is some higher purpose to our lives. The thought that life, or the experience we call life, is a relentless evolutionary process in which we play a hugely insignificant part feels unbearably lonely. It's not for nothing that existentialists, nihilists and hermits are perceived as miserable buggers. If you look at your navel for long enough you can convince yourself that it is the entrance to a bottomless pit. Even hellfire and damnation have the consolation of making you feel necessary, if only for the odd roasting.

I have never had the comfort of religion in a formal sense, but have, as long as I can remember, had a sense of something 'other', like a distant echo or the fragment of a half-remembered tune. The background noise of life makes real thinking a lottery, and those of us with the mental focus of kittens find it easier to wear the robes of having thought, rather than doing actual thinking. That is why so many people have opinions about everything. Depending on which books and newspapers you read, television, radio or films you watch or listen to, it is easy within a fairly short time to have formed opinions about most things, and in many cases to hold them so strongly as to defend them almost unto death.

By the same measure it is easy to isolate a whole raft of issues for which there are a range of views that you could not possibly entertain, because to do so would render the other opinions you have inconsistent. Consistency is what we strive for. So while we like to think of ourselves as individual juries holding up all the evidence under close scrutiny, weighing it and then pronouncing judgement, the truth is a long way from this. The truth is that most of us hold up the evidence that fits our view of the world and find the arguments we need to consolidate it, rather than question it.

We, the jury, demand evidence, yet on almost any subject you care to mention, from immigration to population control, from nuclear power to ASBOs (anti-social behaviour orders), the evidence is not what we want: we want the proof that our opinions are factually sound or at least capable of underpinning our 'belief'. At Eden we hold a series of concerts every summer under the banner of The Eden Sessions. Last year we carried out a small experiment as an entertainment. We printed up a range of questions on cards and invited the public to fill them in. The first batch were very light: "You will be shot tomorrow and tonight you will have your last dance; what tune would you choose?" Alternatively: "You can put three things into a space rocket, never to return to Earth; what would they be?". There were a dozen such questions and thousands filled them in. Interestingly people were even more curious about the answers of others than their own. Buoyed by the success of this we came up with a new question which turned out to be total dynamite: "What do you hold strong opinions about, that you know nothing about?" All around the site you could see people talking about this and many I spoke to felt deeply troubled as it dawned on them that some of their most cherished opinions had no foundation in their own experience or thought.

WESTERN SOCIETY IS AT a crossroads. We have lived through agricultural, industrial and post-industrial revolutions. We are now supposed to be living in the knowledge economy. The Commons have all been colonised (or just about). Common land was enclosed, industrial processes and then ideas were patented and now life itself is being patented. Individual or corporate ownership is everything. The Commons are dead except in mid-ocean. This is the reason behind our economic miracle and why there are so many reasons to be happy about the future. Technology and intellectual property in harness will save the world and liberate us from our chains. The problem is that in our hearts we know that creativity and technological development are responses to markets - to consumption.

We also know that the engine of the market is growth and that growth is only possible if we can keep ourselves in a constant state of dissatisfaction through the marketing of innovation to make us hungry for the next thing. Innovation is in fact, with a few exceptions, the agent of dissatisfaction at the present. It has to be. What an irony, then, that with the rush to ownership comes the fall from grace. The public no longer trust scientists or companies to tell them the truth, believing that there are vested interests at work. Darwin didn't have share options and nor did Alexander Fleming. Is it any wonder that public debate over issues such as genetic modification, organic farming, stem cell research and so on should be so coloured by distrust? The 'Public Good' is perceived to be under threat.

"While science can lead us towards truth, only the imagination can give us meaning" - so C. S. Lewis said. Imagination holds the key. Almost imperceptibly over the last two years I have sensed a growing unease across all sections of society at the impact of human action on the planet. No longer is it just environmentalists or enlightened individuals and companies calling for action to halt the activities causing so much destruction of the environment around the world. It is a popular refrain. For me the interesting thing is that the type of debate has changed significantly. That is not to say that the technological fixes for lower-emission energy, sustainable extraction of resources and so on are not argued in public along scientific lines, but increasingly there is an almost spiritual belief in our having angered 'the Gods'. Where Asterix the Gaul would fear the sky falling on his head, we fear extreme weather and poisoned oceans. And this time it's personal; it's our fault.

It is no accident that politicians have suddenly reawakened to the environment debate. They thought it wasn't an election winner - because it wasn't. But almost overnight the realisation has dawned that this isn't an issue that is going away and more importantly it is an issue on which history will judge them. The Health Service, education, defence, law and order and so on are cultural or social responses to prevailing human conditions. The penny has dropped that the environment could undermine all these and life itself. With so much private fear politicians can feel confident of being able to take unpopular measures in the name of the common good, sure in the knowledge that very soon that common good will be beyond question. It is about harnessing the spirit of war in peace time - and at war things become simple.

ONE OF THE MOST powerful pieces I have read is by the Anglo-Nigerian writer Ben Okri, who says: "Stories are the secret reservoir of values; change the stories individuals and nations live by and tell themselves, and you change the individuals and nations . . . Nations and peoples are largely the stories they feed themselves. If they tell themselves stories that are lies, they will suffer the future consequences of those lies. If they tell themselves stories that face their own truths, they will free their own histories for future flowerings."

Changes are happening all around us. Five years ago you bought eggs; then you bought eggs from free-range chickens; now you buy free-range organic eggs in biodegradable cartons. The story is about chickens and eggs, but it is also about you. Your purchase is telling the world about your care for animal husbandry and the environment. For 'eggs' read any product you could care to name. The revolution is taking hold and the revolution is about using your wallet as the weapon of your personality. It will not be long before there is a real 'tipping point' and the market will succumb wholesale to the better world philosophy. Why? Because it's not just middle-class woolly sentiment; it is turning into a movement of almost spiritual intensity where the individual doesn't want to let careless spending cost lives (to make a doggerel wartime joke of it).

We are indeed the sum of the stories we tell ourselves about ourselves, and the stories we want to tell are about the dawning of a new civilisation based on a simple concept, 'working with the grain of nature': about sustainable living and wholesomeness. This is the world we want to be judged on wishing for, rather than to be judged as pigs feeding at the trough of thoughtless consumption, because here the sky will almost certainly fall on our heads.

SCIENCE AND COMMERCE have led us to this place, but a blind belief that they can, on their own, lead us out will be the end of us. Many people sense this yet feel bashful at expressing it at the risk of appearing idealistic and romantic. This is to misunderstand the nature of the task ahead. This is not a time for burning incense and navel-gazing; nor is it a time to compete head to head with corporate values. It is a time to actively build things, make things, create new types of institution that are capable of adapting quickly to change that work with the grain of nature and that don't mess it up. This is not anti-capitalist: it is common sense and genuinely innovative and will, in its pursuit of the Common Good, create a whole new range of commercial drivers which are based not on wastefulness but on the intelligent husbandry of resources.

So, like that fragment of a half-remembered tune I talked about earlier, I can hear something, and it's big - very, very big. It is a seismic change caused by circumstances now almost beyond our control, the threat of which may yet herald the most fundamental shifts in our civilisation. It makes me cheerful, because in truth I have always felt ambivalent about humans bringing about their own demise, feeling that if we do, we deserve what's coming to us and that the use of the word *'sapiens'* to describe us is deeply funny. No; in a strange way I am looking forward to the smell of intellectual cordite as we capture the spirit of war in a time of peace. It feels like a battle worth fighting that will have many stories to tell.

Tim Smit was an archaeologist and a record-producer/composer before embarking on the award-winning restoration of The Lost Gardens of Heligan and thereafter becoming the creator and co-founder of the Eden Project in Cornwall, UK.

A RADICAL REALIST
JONATHON PORRITT

EDGING CLOSER TO MELTDOWN

I believe there is still 'a window' during which time the actions we take could still ward off ecological and social collapse.

THIS ISN'T AN EASY time to be offering a personal reflection on forty years of environmental engagement. More and more people whose work I respect are now out there saying it's almost certainly too late, in that we have already crossed a number of critical thresholds on climate change and ecosystem degradation. If they are correct, and the still-tentative practice of sustainable development is summarily replaced (in James Lovelock's phrase) by the politics of "sustainable retreat" (where sustainable behaviours are imposed upon us, against our natural inclination, on account of ecological necessity and the threat of even worse things just around the corner), then it's basically 'game over' for environmentalism as we know it today. The deep irony of having won the argument only to see that we are still losing the world is horribly painful.

I'm not in that apocalyptic place myself - yet. I believe there is still 'a window' during which time the actions we take could still ward off ecological and social collapse. And I believe the environment movement still has the pivotal role to play in helping to deliver that kind of 'soft landing' for humankind.

That will come as no surprise to readers of *Resurgence*. Whatever has been achieved by way of progress on environmental issues over the last forty years has come about primarily because of environmental organisations and committed individuals. And we shouldn't underestimate the gains made over the last forty years - on air and water quality, on bathing waters, on protected areas and biodiversity, and so on. Nor should we underestimate the impact on public awareness: in-depth surveys in all OECD (Organisation for Economic Co-operation and Development) countries show substantial and gently rising levels of deep concern.

In that context, most environmentalists today may well be cynical about the much-hyped 'greening' of the UK Conservative Party under the leadership of David Cameron. But they should really be celebrating the media interest this has generated, stimulating competition between the mainstream parties to demonstrate their green credentials, and the sense that this is now genuinely mainstream.

We have been here before, of course - with Margaret Thatcher's (albeit very brief!) green period in the late 1980s, and the huge vote for the Green Party in the 1989 European Election. This time, however, it feels different, not least because public perceptions of climate change are adding a completely different dimension to the debate. But will it be any more durable this time around?

AT WHICH POINT, we have to bring on the debate about the future of the environment movement itself! I got into a lot of trouble with some of my colleagues when my book *Capitalism As If The World Matters* came out last year and the media chose to focus on concerns I raised in it about contemporary environmentalism. Those concerns were hardly that radical: however convincing the *scientific* case made by environmentalists about the need for urgent and far-reaching change in the face of gathering ecological crises, the *popular* case has yet to be made. The fact that change is incontrovertibly necessary does not necessarily make it desirable to people affected directly by that change. And that's really where the focus now needs to be: how to make it both compelling *and* attractive.

This debate has yet to ignite here in the UK. In the US, it has been fizzing away since 2004, with environmentalists arguing passionately about the language they use, the core precepts that lie behind their movement, the balance between top down and bottom up, and the potential for bringing together a much broader coalition of progressive causes to take on the neo-conservatives - not so much through the issues themselves, but through clear moral repositioning and a direct appeal to people's core values. Many now believe that an excessively technocratic, regulation-driven approach to protecting the environment has allowed the neo-conservatives to win the battle for people's hearts and minds, appealing unapologetically to their sense of themselves as fair, hard-working, entrepreneurial citizens - oppressed rather than liberated by their environmental protectors.

All this may have something to do with the nature of the environment movement in the United States. Robert Brulle's analysis of the eighty-seven organisations that make up the core of the US movement highlights some startling issues: 90% of environmental activity in those organisations is oriented around just two principal concerns - wildlife protection and landscape conservation. As he says, "it is difficult to dispute the claim that the wellbeing of people has consistently been an under-emphasized facet of American environmental activism." Drawing on the fascinating work of George Lakoff, who has written extensively on the importance of progressive politicians 'framing' things in the right way, he goes on to assert that, "to be politically affective, progressives need to develop a simple unified frame that resonates with existing identities and unifies various political proposals."

The reluctance of the US movement to talk about equity issues both *within the US* (in terms of 'environmental justice' - the well-established phenomenon of environmental externalities impacting disproportionately on less well-off communities and households) and *globally* (in terms of the 'race to the bottom' caused by footloose US capital seeking out profit-maximising deals in countries with lower labour and environmental standards), has left most environmental organisations marooned in a zone of utter irrelevance as global economic forces negate the small victories won on the battleground of narrow, technically determined environmentalism.

It's a different story here in the UK and in other European countries. From its inception, Friends of the Earth has brought radical perspectives to bear on the core environmental proposition - around health, work, communities, economic development, and so on. Greenpeace has campaigned with as much vigour for a world free of nuclear weapons as it has for a world free of nuclear reactors. WWF occasionally goes beyond its focus on the world's "charismatic megafauna" to take up the cudgels for the human species - as with its current campaign on toxic chemicals and their impact on human health.

BUT ARE WE *currently* targeting resources in the right way? Have we really come up with an effective model of social change? For all sorts of valid historical reasons, the culture of many environmental organisations has been shaped by the campaigns they have been obliged to wage *against* governments and multinational companies. The collective psyche of our movement is still oppositional and, more often than not, confrontational. The finger of blame wags wearily on.

Interestingly, however, it's rarely pointed at individual citizens: it's the politicians that represent them, or the businesses that provide for their every want or need, that are put in the dock. When did you last hear an environmental organisation castigate ordinary people in the UK for leading such greedy, self-obsessed, unhealthy, lazy, indifferent or even callous lives? Or (to be a bit more positive about it!), what percentage of the total spend deployed by environmental organisations in the UK is devoted to changing people's behaviours rather than changing the minds of legislators or business leaders?

Not much, is the answer. But that may well be because environmental organisations simply can't afford to hurl hard-earned (usually charitable) money into the bottomless pit of public education. So, what if government itself provided the money, business provided the access, and non-governmental organisations the content and integrity? That would have been unthinkable even a couple of years ago, but as the planet literally melts down in front of us, expect only the unexpected in terms of innovation, inspiration and *real* leadership.

Jonathon Porritt is Founder Director of Forum for the Future <www.forumforthefuture.org.uk> and Chair of the UK Sustainable Development Commission <www.sdcommission.org.uk>.

THE ECO-ENTREPRENEUR
JOHN ELKINGTON

THE BUSINESS END
OF ALL THIS

I seem to be coming full circle,
back to 'small is beautiful'.

IT'S ALMOST IMPOSSIBLE to say "No" to Satish Kumar, Editor of
Resurgence. Like monsoons and the Amazon, he's a force of nature. And
it was harder still when he was cranking up to celebrate the fortieth
anniversary of *Resurgence*, to which I have been a proud, if erratic, con-
tributor. But his request - that I write about how business has evolved
over the past forty years and where it might go over the next forty,
all while "making it your personal story" - was a typically tough
challenge. And the image that first sprang to mind?

Well, it was Canadian Nick Parker, co-founder of the Cleantech
Venture Network, telling several hundred hard-nosed venture capitalists in San Francisco a few weeks earlier that my seventh book, *The*

Green Capitalists, had saved his soul. It did so, apparently, by showing that it is possible to save the environment and make a profit. The book appeared in 1987, also the year during which we founded SustainAbility and - six months later - the Brundtland Commission published its report, *Our Common Future*.

Suddenly, sustainable development was headed into the mainstream. Instead of aiming to save people's souls, however, it seeks to protect the conditions of life for future generations of all species. Just as well, really, since I'm truly not in the soul-saving business.

During the Cold War years, and with a father who had been a Battle of Britain pilot, I suppose it was inevitable that my main interest in the products of industry (apart from water pistols and bicycles) was aircraft. Away at school, I amused myself by writing to aircraft companies to get catalogues and photographs of their latest machines. They humoured me, but in the process, unwittingly, I learned key lessons about technological evolution. And when the environmental movement took off around the same time, that early interest in innovation powerfully shaped my odyssey into the worlds of business and environment.

There were other stepping stones, too. For example, having begun working in the environmental field in 1972, I also began to write for *New Scientist*, a role which enabled me to see at first hand what companies were doing in such areas as ecosystem restoration and environmental impact assessment. That led to my being invited to be one of the founders in 1978 (with Max Nicholson, also one of the founders of WWF) of Environmental Data Services (ENDS), and that led, after various peregrinations, to SustainAbility.

BUT IF YOU MOVE COUNTER-CURRENT, you should expect resistance. I well recall being told by several environmentalist friends during the 1980s that the only way to deal with companies was to tie them down with regulations, like so many Gullivers snared by Lilliputians. Even then, this notion made me uncomfortable. I knew from school that things we are forced to do engage us less power-fully than things we are helped to discover for ourselves. And that belief drove my early work and writing, although many early suc-cesses were accidents, as when our book *The Green Consumer Guide* appeared in 1988, selling around a million copies and helping trig-ger massive pressure on companies and simultaneously creating a counter-intuitive magnet effect, with major companies queuing up to work with us - rather than shunning us as the troublemakers we undoubtedly were.

Later, in 1994, we tried to work out what had been going on around us. We mapped a series of waves of public pressure on busi-ness. Wave 1, the 'Limits' pressure wave, built from the 1960, with early events including the founding of Amnesty and WWF in 1961, and the publication of Jane Jacobs' *The Death and Life of Great American Cities* in 1961 and of Rachel Carson's *Silent Spring* in 1962. The wave accelerated towards the end of the decade, peaking from 1969 to 1973. Through the mid-1970s, a wave of environmental legislation swept across the industrial world. Most companies went into defen-sive, compliance mode.

I had enthusiastically experimented with the 'small is beautiful' movement, working briefly at a number of alternative technology test beds, but most eventually imploded. Small in a big-is-better world proved difficult to sustain. Downwave 1 overlapped this period of experimentation, running from 1974 to 1987. Acid rain had a major impact on EU politics in the early 1980s, but this was largely a period of conservative politics, with attempts to roll back environmental legislation. I found myself on advisory boards in organisations like the UK Central Electricity Generating Board.

Wave 2, the 'Green' pressure wave, really took off in 1987-8. Issues such as ozone depletion and rainforest destruction helped fuel the growth of the green consumer movement. The peak of that wave ran from 1988 to 1991, with Downwave 2 following in 1991. The UN Earth Summit in Rio in 1992 somewhat delayed the downwave, triggering spikes in media coverage of climate change and biodiversity, but against a falling trend in public concern. The trends were not all down, however. There were further spikes through the mid- and late 1990s, driven by controversies around companies such as Shell, Monsanto and Nike, and by public concerns - at least in Europe - about 'mad cow disease' and genetically modified foods. In 1994, I coined the term 'triple bottom line' to describe exactly the sort of complex challenges that such companies were now facing.

Wave 3, the 'Globalisation' pressure wave, began in 1999. Protests against the World Trade Organization, the World Bank, the International Monetary Fund, the G8, the World Economic Forum and other institutions spotlighted the critical role of governments and international institutions in promoting - or hindering - sustainable development. In my 2001 book *The Chrysalis Economy* I predicted that from 2000 to 2030 we would see an increasingly convulsive period of 'creative destruction', with many unsustainable industries heading into extinction. Uncomfortably ahead of its time, the book bombed - but increasingly it looks prescient.

Downwave 3 began in 2002 and will likely run for five to eight years. Paradoxically, given the Bush regime's recalcitrance on such issues, the emerging wave is currently most obvious in the US. This is where the 'cleantech' revolution Parker and his colleagues are heralding is mainly surfacing. Focusing on everything from environmental clean-up through solar photovoltaics to nanomaterials, the

Cleantech Venture Network team says that over US$8 billion has been invested in this area since 1999 in North America alone. And it forecasts that investment will climb to an average US$3.9 billion a year between 2006 and 2009, putting cleantech ahead of the semiconductor sector.

BUT THAT'S ONLY part of the picture. Donning my pessimist's hat, I foresee that by 2046 world population may have reached nine billion - though I very much doubt it - and humanity will be learning to live with the consequences of abrupt climate change, massive pandemics and new forms of terrorism. Dark clouds, though, often have silver linings. As China globalises and its horrendous environmental and resource issues begin to bite savagely it could become an incubator of 'green' technologies. In that hope, we are boosting our own work in such emerging economies.

Given how long it takes to turn around the large 'supertanker' companies we mainly work with, probably the most exciting thing on our horizon is our new $1- million, three-year grant from the Skoll Foundation, set up by one of the founders of eBay. This will help support our evolving work with social entrepreneurs. Oddly, I increasingly feel I'm coming full circle, back into the 'small is beautiful' space, but this time with potentially useful connections back into the worlds of business and finance - and with a very different perspective on the need to ensure that such experiments replicate and scale to meet global needs.

Finally, donning my optimist's hat, I see a future in which, by the time *Resurgence* is fifty and - other forces of nature permitting - I am an entrepreneurial sixty-seven, I am still unable to say "No" to Satish, the fourth pressure wave has peaked, and an extraordinary new landscape of sustainability-focused innovation and market opportunity beckons. Though it's quite a stretch, both *Resurgence* and the roles of business have mutated to such an extent that *Resurgence* 3.0 is required browsing for venture capitalists, investment bankers, financial analysts and corporate board members. Imagine!

John Elkington is co-founder and Chief Entrepreneur at SustainAbility <www.sustainability.com> and blogs at <www.johnelkington.com>. He is co-author of The Green Consumer Guide and author of Cannibals with Forks and The Chrysalis Economy.

LOW-CARBON FUTURE

No more compromise: I say we need
Greens in governments NOW!

FORTY YEARS FROM now, society is unrecognisable. The consequences of global climate change and sweeping democratisation and localisation have changed almost every aspect of our lives, from where and how we live and work to the food we eat and the way we spend our leisure time.

It's 2046, and a Green Party government has been re-elected in the UK - joining those in power across much of the EU. The Prime Minister gives her acceptance speech in the capital, Birmingham. (The seat of government moved north a few years back, to an area in need of urban regeneration, after rising sea levels repeatedly breached the Thames barrier, flooding much of Westminster and rendering it unsafe.)

The UN's revised turn-of-the-century call for an 80% cut in

global greenhouse-gas emissions by 2050 was met five years ago, thanks largely to the sharp escalation in fossil-fuel prices as peak oil took hold in 2012. This fuel crisis drove sweeping improvements in energy conservation, renewable generation, and the free transfer of technology to the developing world as eco-aid administered by a reformed, democratic UN (which celebrated its centenary last year).

Our communities are safer: we live in well-designed, insulated, warm homes, eat more locally grown, organic food, enjoy greater security, are healthier and live longer. Few of us drive a car any more: since oil prices escalated most of us have switched to trams and trains, creating the cash to drive the UK's biggest single investment in public transport infrastructure.

PERHAPS THIS IS naive in its unbridled optimism. Perhaps we'll miss our CO_2-reduction targets, forgotten in a world of conflict over ever scarcer dwindling reserves of oil. The UN could stagnate further, in the face of increasingly unilateralist US and UK governments - China and India could retreat into war over economic dominance of a region racked by starvation and disease as its rich get richer and its poor poorer.

The future is in our hands. It is becoming increasingly clear that the next forty years will be the most crucial period in the history of humankind. In climate change we face our biggest ever challenge to life as we know it: the decisions we make over the next forty years might determine the very survival of our species. Now is a critical moment to reflect on the lessons of the last forty.

Forty years ago there was no green movement in the UK - let alone internationally - that we would recognise today. The Campaign for Nuclear Disarmament (CND) had been formed eight years earlier, and WWF in 1961, but Greenpeace, Friends of the Earth and even the Green Party wouldn't emerge for another few years.

The political context was hostile to environmentalism, and even revolutionary voices like Rachel Carson's were drowned out of mainstream public discourse - but the steady flow of new information about the impact of our lives on the world around us led thousands to change their lives, take direct environmental action, explore new technologies and social models and join like-minded people. Over the years, *Resurgence* has told many of their stories.

But the nascent green movement in the UK and US, and, later, internationally, was depoliticised from the start. Campaigns to alleviate poverty, stop war, save endangered species or build sustainable communities flourished outside the realms of electoral democracy. As non-governmental organisations (NGOs) shaped particular campaigns, they sought, and sometimes won, support from existing political parties (who were naturally suspicious of any attempt by Greens to win power themselves).

Green parties began contesting elections in the 1970s (the Australian Green Party was the first, in 1972, with the UK Greens' predecessor People in 1974). However, without the explicit support of the NGOs and the wider green movement, and often vilified as advocates of 'hair-shirt asceticism', they failed to make much electoral mark until 1981, when nine members entered the Belgian parliament and - with even greater fanfare - two years later when twenty-eight members of *Die Grünen* were elected to the German Bundestag.

I confess I remember these events only dimly. In the early 1980s, I was graduating from poetry to the peace and women's movements. For me, that was the start of a far greater political awareness and, in particular, a strong pacifist conviction and a commitment to CND. But it wasn't until 1986, when I stumbled across Jonathon Porritt's book *Seeing Green*, that I realised that all my deepest concerns - peace, social justice and protecting our fragile environment - were intertwined and connected through the damage being done by the global spread of 20th-century-style capitalism, and that there was a political party - albeit, as Petra Kelly put it, an "anti-party party" - which shared them.

I put my life on hold to join the Green Party, and for several years worked as its Press Officer, determined to increase media coverage of its radical, inspiring and increasingly urgent message.

Those years saw pioneering Green parties elected to national parliaments in Austria, Italy, Luxembourg, Portugal and Sweden. Further afield, two Green senators won seats in the Australian parliament. At the same time, a groundswell of Greens was moving into local government in almost every Western European country, and around the world not only were local Green groups multiplying in number but their activities were also becoming more influential.

In 1989, the British Greens saw their greatest ever electoral success, securing almost 15% of the vote in the European Election - trumping the Liberals into fourth place. But the UK's archaic first-past-the-post system meant we were denied even a single MEP. The despondency this caused, together with a lack of resources which left the party unprepared to deal with a sudden (but all-too brief) upsurge of new members and interest, would prove catalysts for internal arguments, management crises and, ultimately, a haemorrhage of support.

The Green Party picked up the pieces in the 1990s and underwent an electorally focused transformation which saw a modest rise in its electoral fortunes. I had a small share of it, being elected in 1993 - after three attempts -to Oxfordshire County Council.

As a councillor I developed my personal links with campaigners and NGOs, and we shared a feeling of political optimism. By 1998 the Greens were coalition partners in the governments of Germany and Finland, and in 1999 I was elected as one of the UK's first two Green Party MEPs, after securing more than 8% of the vote across South-East England - a result impossible without the implicit support of the wider green movement, both locally and internationally.

Internationally, to achieve the spectacular high of twenty-five Green Parties, represented in eleven parliaments, in less than ten years was no small achievement. Not only that, but by the end of the 1990s there were Greens in five coalition governments in the EU, making it the fastest-growing political movement ever.

THOSE WERE HEADY days indeed - but they were destined not to last. As we in the UK were learning to work more closely with greens outside the party, Greens in Germany were grappling with the pressure of having to work more closely with government partners outside the party. The party's support for the Afghan War in 2001 spelt the beginning of the end for the German 'Red-Green Alliance' - and of Greens in coalition governments in Europe.

From having representatives in five EU governments in 2001, the Greens now boast none, most having been forced from office after losing the support of a wider green movement and bearing responsibility for the unsustainable policies and decisions of their larger coalition partners (the Finns having honourably resigned from government in protest over nuclear power).

This has led to a fractured debate within Green parties and the wider green movement: are we more effective working inside governments or outside? What level of support is a precondition for operating within coalitions? Is it more effective to shout oppositionally from the rooftops, or quietly tinker with policies from within?

105

Ironically, it is those parties with better roots in the campaigning and NGO communities, in France and Germany, which have tended to embrace coalition as a route to immediate influence - and have been punished for it by greens feeling betrayed by their compromises.

SO WHILE I put my hopes for the future firmly with the world's Green parties - since none of the mainstream parties are coming remotely close to an understanding of the policy agenda that we so urgently need - it is clear that we must learn the lessons of the past forty years. In particular, that we must engage and synthesise with the wider international green movement, and avoid coalitions with larger parties until we are strong enough to resist unacceptable compromises.

It has been said by some that electoral success came too early and too easily to some of the European Green parties: that having to learn on the job is not always the best way of producing the best policies and strategies. However, we don't have the luxury of a long apprenticeship. As greater awareness of the fast-approaching collapse of the world's ecosystem grows, it brings with it not only the urgency for action, but the hope that growing concerns will translate into a thoroughgoing revolution in attitudes and in political support. Greens need to seize every opportunity to describe the positive benefits of a low-carbon future, and promote the real, everyday benefits of living in a Green society.

The international green movement, and more specifically, the Green parties which have sprung up around the world to represent it, have achieved much: attracting millions of votes and returning Greens to shape policy in parliaments and town and city halls across the world.

But there is so much more to do - if my dream of the world in

2046 is to be any more than a dream, we need Greens in government now to ensure its smooth delivery.

As more and more people realise that we face global devastation, and that Green solutions deliver not hair shirts and dry muesli but stronger communities, warmer homes, better jobs, and greater hope for the future, more and more Greens will be elected, and will achieve majorities - and we will fulfil our role as the political wing of a wider green movement that will be spreading ever more rapidly worldwide.

Caroline Lucas is Green Party MEP for South-East England, Vice-President of the RSPCA and Stop the War Coalition, a National Council member of the Campaign for Nuclear Disarmament and a Director of the International Forum on Globalization. She was first elected to the European Parliament in 1999, and is a member of the Parliameant's Trade and Environment Committees. Before her election, she worked as a Policy Adviser for Oxfam, and has published widely on globalisation and environment issues.

THE SOCIAL REVOLUTIONARY
ALAN SIMPSON

THE LONG
AND WINDING ROAD

Climate change will, I believe, be the trigger that
brings 'corporate feudalism' to an end.

I GREW UP with John, Paul, George, Ringo and *Resurgence*. It just
took me a while to catch up with the seeds of exciting irreverence
that *Resurgence* was to plant in my life. The magazine's explorations
turned conventional ideas about economy and environment upside
down. It brought the same creative turbulence into thoughts about
the physical and metaphysical world as the Beatles had done to my
musical world.

In truth, I was still kicking a ball about the streets of Liverpool
when *Resurgence* was born. Your first issue followed on from the
posthumous publication of Rachel Carson's *The Sense of Wonder* and
Ralph Nader's *Unsafe at Any Speed* - an indictment of the US automotive

industry. Four years earlier, when Carson's *Silent Spring* was published the reaction of farmers, agronomists and the agro-chemical industry was to accuse her of wanting to starve people by banning the use of pesticides. We were a long way from living in tune with nature.

At the time, me and my football were oblivious to all such arguments and it took me until the late 1960s and early 1970s to begin to catch up. What I want to reflect on, though, is the sense of the time in which *Resurgence* began and how it relates to where we are now.

IT IS WITH A sense of pride rather than apology that I freely admit to being a child of the 1960s. The time brought with it a gift of optimism that has never left me. No single individual or social movement can lay claim to the spirit of internationalism and environmentalism that burst into life. It was a spirit that found a voice in anti-war protests, pro-democracy movements, liberation theology and new approaches to common ownership and industrial democracy. In an era in which the personal became the political, a carnival of musicians, poets and writers were somehow able to embrace the dreams of a generation who wanted to live differently upon the planet.

The environmental agenda began slowly and in the margins, often more concerned with opting out than opting in, or being oppositional rather than propositional. By 1969 Neil Armstrong had set foot on the moon, twenty million people had died in severe famine in China, and Friends of the Earth was formed. Two years later Greenpeace arrived too, but my recollection of the time was of efforts going into pollution protests and demands for increased aid to tackle "Third World poverty", rather than of demands for systematic change in our political ecology.

By the early 1970s we were running a community food co-op from our garage and were involved in setting up urban farms. But these were more about awareness and access to fresh food than about ecological footprinting. We still had a long way to go before catching up with Italy's Slow Food Movement or the concept of food miles. Ivan Illich's *Energy and Equity* was the only book I can recall that questioned the energy inputs that underpinned modern life and I can still remember the buzz of excitement when listening to him (and then Paolo Freire) at meetings crowded out by those of us who thought we were part of an unstoppable social revolution. Hindsight teaches you that progress is cyclical rather than linear, that we often learn nothing from history other than how to make the same mistakes on a bigger scale, and that humanity brings to the planet a never-ending struggle between individual greed and social solidarity.

By the mid-seventies I had already accepted that I would only ever admit to being a 'lapsed' economist. It would be unfair to blame this on E. F. Schumacher because I had already run into serious differences about economic theory and had started to feel that most of the theories made more sense if you stood them on their head or reversed them. Schumacher's *Small is Beautiful* simply blew everything sideways. His notion of Buddhist economics stopped me in my tracks. He redefined the whole purpose of economic life as an ethical triptych - three connected panels in which we live out the relationship between ourselves and our creative possibilities, between ourselves and others, and between ourselves and the planet. His ideas closed the gap that often seemed to sit uncomfortably between socialism and environmentalism.

IT WAS 'SOD'S LAW' that I was to discover this at a time when the world was heading on a trajectory from Fordism to post-Fordism, and on to corporate globalisation. In truth, today's globalisation is really corporate feudalism. The accelerating exploitation of people and the planet requires a massive transfer of civic rights to underpin it.

Capital and corporations are given unfettered rights beyond the reach of any enjoyed by citizens. They have the freedom to go where they like, do what they like and leave when they want. States are told it is illegal, under World Trade Organization (WTO) rules, to restrict the movement of capital or the freedom of companies to take over (or abandon) whatever part of the economy they like. Lone-parent companies can misbehave as much as they like, but lone-parent families are to be disciplined, stigmatised, subjected to curfews or anti-social behaviour orders and made the subject of a welter of state legislation to 'protect society'. Corporate feudalism demands that states micro-manage the lives of their citizens rather than macro-manage their economies.

It will all end the way that feudalism did. The difference today is that climate change crises are the most likely triggers for social revolutions that will bring corporate feudalism to an end. Explaining this will be the next stage of the *Resurgence* journey. Filling the process with hope and inspiration will be the litmus test of the magazine's relevance to our troubled times. The same can be said of my own journey.

I NO LONGER BELIEVE it is possible to stop the planet drifting into deep environmental crisis. Climate change is already happening and its impact will be exponential. My optimism about changing the world for the better has shifted to an optimism that we can still manage our way through catastrophic upheavals, in ways that allow us to live better lives - by living more lightly upon the planet. It all depends on environmentalism becoming the centre stage of economics rather than an activity on the margins.

The good news is that never before in human history have we had the tools at hand to transform life for the mass of humanity rather than for the few. The difficulty is that it requires a revolution in the soul of our societies in order to unleash the transformation. The big idea for the 21st century is that all of the answers are to be found in the absence of bigness. It's a bit of a bummer for today's corporate giants, but tomorrow's solutions will be found in networks and systemic interdependencies, not in global behemoths.

Climate change brings with it inseparable crises in food security, water management and energy supply. Managing our way through these crises will require a wholly new approach to systems thinking. The challenge to environmental movements is whether we can lead the way in the politics and economics of sustainability. Big national power-generation and national 'grid' energy-distribution systems have to be replaced by decentralised energy networks. The built environment has to become a source of energy generation more than energy consumption. Market price mechanisms need to pay more for the sustainable energy put into energy networks than the cost of taking energy from the system.

So too with water storage, use and retention. If flash flooding and drought are to be features within the same season, the challenge is to see how the built environment can respond to both, as sources of potential energy, and how it can store from one in order to provide during the other. The case for local food systems taking precedence over global markets will have to be recalibrated, not simply in terms of food miles, carbon impact and producer accountability, but also in terms of water sequestration by the richest in the North from the poorest in the South.

The internationalism of our age will not be found in an expansion of world trade. It will emerge from the cargoes of intellectual contraband that we exchange freely (without royalties or patents) on how best to survive. This is where my own journey has brought me to.

SYMBOLICALLY, I LOOK back to my childhood and believe that its greatest gifts were (and are) embodied in the Blood Transfusion Service. The sociologist Richard Titmuss described it as "the Gift Relationship". We go and give blood as an act of social solidarity. When doing so, none of us asks how much we are to be paid, how much we have in our account or what interest it has earned. We give into a common process in the belief that it is the best way of meeting our common needs. Countries that have marketised the process turn citizens into commodities, cheapen every part of life they touch, and add to social insecurities.

So it is with the planet. Selfishly, the rich now need the poor to act ethically if we are all to survive. The new 'gift relationship' will require free transfers from North to South, from rich to poor, of the technologies for sustainable survival. A new economics will place the right to produce for domestic food security well before presumptions of globalised trade. The urgency of making these changes is just 'Schumacher with attitude', *Resurgence* with an agenda.

So, *Resurgence*, forty years on and the message is still the same. As the lads said in 1970, "the long and winding road . . . always leads me here, leads me to your door." There is just a greater urgency about opening it along with everyone else's.

Alan Simpson is one of that rare breed of MPs who are still happy to be identified as socialists and ecologists. When he entered parliament in 1992 New Statesman dubbed him "the man most likely to come up with ideas": the kiss of death for a career in New Labour. He has won the Green Futures Environmental Politician of the Year award and turned a derelict shell into an eco dream home. He campaigns against fuel poverty, GM crops, globalisation and privatisation and continues to play tennis, football and cricket.

THE ETHICAL ECONOMIST
DAVID BOYLE

IN SEARCH OF AUTHENTICITY

I think ethical consumerism is a spiritual act.

CAN REMEMBER the 1966 general election, but only just. It was the first time I had run across such a thing before - I was eight - and I decided I was a Conservative on the grounds that it was the only party not beginning with L.

But of all the events of those years - the World Cup, flower power - what I really remember was the 'I'm Backing Britain' campaign.

It is true that this was actually 1968, but the Union Jack posters and the excruciating campaign song by Bruce Forsyth remain etched on my brain. Other people spent the sixties at Woodstock or on the hippy trail; I think I was just "backing Britain". The country was generally agreed to be in a mess. Harold Wilson had devalued the pound, blaming the "gnomes of Zurich" - an early form of globalisation, no doubt.

'I'm Backing Britain' rather lost its glamour when it was revealed that the campaign T-shirts were actually made in Portugal, and it was soon forgotten. But I suppose, 'Backing Britain' was a way of using our consumer spending power to achieve political ends.

Leap nearly two decades, to the publication of John Elkington and Julia Hailes' *Green Consumer Guide*. At the time, I was editor of a magazine called *Town & Country Planning*, and searching for the missing element that had the potential to solve the environmental crisis.

I became concerned about the threat of nuclear energy while I was at university, and shifted my political allegiance to the Liberals - despite their initial L - who were then fighting a losing battle against Sellafield in the House of Commons.

I wrote all the environment stories on my local paper when I was a reporter, but found myself specialising even further, looking for anything which might provide the clue to the missing lever that would green the planet. I eventually decided this was green economics, joined the New Economics Foundation and wrote so many books about money that I became almost sick of the sight of it!

THERE IS NO DOUBT that the birth of green consumerism in 1987 demonstrated to people that they did, after all, have an economic weapon at their disposal in the battle for the planet. And having discovered that weapon, it seemed perverse not to use it. Before the *Green Consumer Guide*, the Church of England could - and did - have shareholdings in the Playboy Channel, because it was a 'good' investment. After the *Guide*, that seemed really rather extraordinary.

What was the point, after all, of us expending so much energy trying to make the world sustainable, if our pension money was invested in British Nuclear Fuels, Exxon or Tesco?

So when people tired of green consuming, as they did for a while, it was the ethical investment movement that led the way back there. That, and people's increasing need for ethical coherence.

Contradictions bother them. There are increasingly few of us who can still follow Keynes' advice to pretend for a while that "foul is useful and fair is not". Now there is £4.2 billion invested ethically in the UK - up from less than £900m in 1989 - and a similar phenomenon is taking place in other areas of the economy. The successes are extraordinary if you look back forty years. The organic food market is growing at the rate of 25% a year, fair trade at 40% a year.

Some products have either squeezed out their unethical competitors or become market leaders in their own right. Who in 1966 had heard of lead-free petrol or free-range eggs? Yet that very success demonstrates the weaknesses of consumerism. It depends on an unsustainable system of semi-monopoly providers to manufacture, import or stock those products in the first place. And it assumes they stay in existence. There's no doubt that green and ethical consumerism isn't enough, but there other reasons why I'm in favour of continuing to try.

First, consumers do have serious power if they act together. I remember publishing an article by the anarchist writer Colin Ward in 1988, looking at how the DIY boom had regenerated thousands of impoverished homes that would have otherwise just been bulldozed by the Government. Now that we are having to face the possibility that governments are actually powerless to stop global warming - and search for some interim alternative - using our spending power is at least an option.

Second, those who believe in nothing but the hidden hand of the market find that green consumers undermine everything they believe in. That is why the market ideologues hate fair trade - it proves there is more to life than price.

Third, it proves to people who have a more spiritual view of the world that they are not alone.

WHEN THE AMERICAN sociologist Paul Ray described what he called 'cultural creatives', he found that they tended to be people who felt almost alone in their values. They felt their opinions were shared just by a handful of close friends. Actually, they seem to account for a quarter of the North American population - and probably a considerably larger proportion in the UK. They may not yet be a majority, but these people have clout if they choose to use it.

I tried to track this phenomenon myself in a book called *Authenticity*, which described the unease people felt about the brave new world predicted for them by information technology corporations and governments alike. In response, they and their friends increasingly want food that is grown somewhere particular, by someone particular. Cafédirect's website now has pictures of some of its growers. Some potato crisp companies give the name of the person who fried the batch in each packet. Lush packaging even has a picture of the employee who made the contents of the box.

That's authentic, or at least if gives the whiff of authenticity. Corporations that produce jeans made in Asian sweatshops where women are beaten if they ask to go to the lavatory will not be able to follow that particular path with their marketing.

These consumers in search of authenticity may not campaign for human rights or saving the whale, but they are enraged by the prospect that they will lose the choice of the authentic option - that a real human doctor or real human teacher might one day be priced beyond them, just as they have lost real human bank managers or often real human shop-keepers.

I remember a New Economics Foundation colleague being bawled at by a Tesco executive around 2001 for suggesting that this process will continue. The ethical revolution has gone as far as it is going, he said - but it clearly hasn't.

117

You can see why it disturbs the supermarkets at least. First they fuel the demand for authenticity with colourful exotics from all over the world. Then that isn't enough, and they have to have fair trade or local produce too, and then - well, what then?

The truth is that what people are now demanding - local healthy, authentic food - is incompatible with modern technocratic delivery systems. There is a fascinating crunch point coming, because the market will provide what they demand - it always does in the end.

I HAVE ONLY recently realised what this demand for authenticity is about. It is a longing for human connection, in a world where corporations and governments are moving slowly towards abolishing it.

It is a reaction to health systems where you never see the same doctor twice. Where heathcare is replaced by a units of intervention, and where education becomes reduced to learning outcomes.

It is a reaction to the shiny one-dimensional world of marketing, where price is the only variable. It is a demand for depth, and depth in our understanding of human nature too.

That's why I have some hope for consumerism. Despite the narrowness of the market, despite the technocratic systems that are engulfing us, it gives us a small way in which we can express some aspects of spirituality and do so every day.

It isn't everything. It certainly isn't the only answer, but it is something. It's a vote, and we should use it..

David Boyle is an associate at the New Economics Foundation and author of The Tyranny of Numbers, The Money Changers and Authenticity. His new book on the imprisonment of Richard the Lionheart is Blondel's Song. <www.david-boyle.co.uk>

THE SEER
SARA PARKIN

LESSONS ON LEADERSHIP

I'm positive that strategic, adaptive leadership will
facilitate truly sustainable development
over the next forty years.

WHAT A YEAR for parties! Forum for the Future is ten, *Resurgence* is forty, and I, to my surprise, am sixty. A timely if terrifying moment to be asked for a personal reflection backwards and forwards about the green movement from the perspective of leadership.

It seems only yesterday I was rocking around the 1960s, enjoying Bob Dylan and the Beatles in Harold Macmillan's "you've never had it so good" world. My parents' generation sacrificed their youth to World War II so when they exhorted mine to enjoy ours we took it very seriously. Before long, however, evidence that our generation would face even bigger challenges seeped into our enjoyment of free education, safe streets and sex, and no job or pension worries. Increasingly, the Cold War shaped the way political leaders ran the world. And it was a very male shape as both sides relaxed into the gang psychology of them and us, recruiting allies, and holding powwows. Meanwhile, people like me stock-piled canned food during the Cuba crisis, took to the streets about American intervention in Vietnam, and watched uneasily as the Berlin Wall went up. We also read about the way global - and local - ecosystems were straining to mop up our waste and pollution (including CO_2 even then). The pile of evidence submitted to the first Earth Summit in 1972 was eleven feet high.

By the time that 'blue marble' image of the Earth taken by Apollo 17 appeared and became an iconic image of the global green movement, I had done a wholesale review of my life goals and was a paid-up campaigner for population, anti-poverty and environmental groups. Motivated by compassion for people (I used to be a nurse) I felt I should devote my life to trying to mitigate the pain of the clash between the aspirations of the human species and the clearly finite capacity of the Earth to support them.

So, like *Resurgence* I am also celebrating forty years of campaigning. The tactics we use may be different, but the direction of travel is the same - which is all that matters - though I remain worried about how much of the green movement forgets how much our campaign is about people. Nature knows how to endure and thrive. It is our species that has lost the plot. For me, sustainable development is about people choosing a path for our progress that is fair and will keep us happy, prosperous and safe for multiple generations. The historical mistake of capitalism and socialism has been to forget that the human story is played out in the natural world. The environment movement is in danger of making the mirror mistake by excluding the wellbeing of people from concerns about the wellbeing of the planet.

POLITICS IS, OF course, about power. And I joined the UK Green

Party in 1977 because I wanted to get green ideas into power. In 1990 I gave a Schumacher Lecture: 'Politics Beyond Power'. My thesis was that there is no such thing. Power does not go away if you ignore it. Someone, somewhere, has got it and it can indeed be a force for good or bad. So how power is given, held to account, removed or relinquished deserves not necessarily a lot of pomp, but certainly much more circumstance.

A couple of years ago, the German Green Party hosted, in Washington, an international seminar on the progress of Green parties since 1983 when *Die Grünen* entered the German parliament. Because of my history in green politics, I was invited to give a global overview. I noted that in 1984 Green parties averaged 3.1% of the vote where they stood in that year's European elections. Twenty years later, they averaged 8.4% of the vote. Even allowing for electoral ups and downs, is struggling to top 10% of the vote after twenty years a strategy worthy of the magnitude of change needed? I hope not, yet I'm hard put to find a Green party with a game plan that will take it to 51% of the vote. Most manifestos read like a 'mission impossible' script recruiting to a minority sport rather than offering an option attractive to the majority. Ambivalence about leadership and power, and poor understanding of the psychology of behaviour change still handicap the performance of Green parties.

During the 1980s I worked with the European Greens to support the green and democratic movement in east Europe. We smuggled scientific papers, photocopiers and friendship across the barbed wire. They knew significant change was coming, because no-one believed food shortages and degrading living conditions were government policy. They knew that the government was out of control. But none of us, including governments either side of the wall, had any idea about how to prepare for the magnitude of change that was

121

coming, or how to manage when it arrived.

Many of my friends discovered the hard way that the leadership attributes needed for dissidence were different from those needed to hold power. Democracy and justice proved not to be default positions for human society, but requiring of diligence and care to install and maintain. Managing change on several levels and across different policy areas at once called on different institutions and very special leadership skills. Yet thinking about the challenges of climate change, or the way the US and UK governments have responded to international terrorism, or even in the way leadership training is done today, I realise that few lessons have been brought forward from the way the Cold War ended.

PREPARING LEADERSHIP TO meet the challenges of the 21st century is at the heart of what Forum for the Future does, with our Leadership for Sustainable Development Masters showing the way. Over the past decade we've graduated over one hundred students who are now making a difference in leadership roles in every sector, sometimes in their own business or social enterprise, and, for me, the next ten years will be about taking to scale the Forum's distinct approach to developing sustainability-literate leadership. Yes, the focus will stay on the new generation of leaders, but as most of the key decisions affecting the next twenty-plus years are likely to be taken by people already in power, we are aware they need to be 'retrofitted' with 'sustainability literacy' as an urgent priority. We ran a pilot elective for twelve students on Applied Sustainability at the London Business School earlier this year. Good feedback from students was accompanied by concern that nothing like it was happening in other courses in what is one of the world's top business schools.

I am actually feeling very positive about the next forty years, even if I am not certain about whether it will be the green movement providing the leadership on sustainable development. There is an entirely welcome competition developing between the Conservative and Labour parties in the UK about who is the greenest of us all, driven by worry about the evidence of climate change and resource shortages as much as a desire for votes. Gordon Brown is talking about a "new synthesis" needed to achieve economic growth, social justice and environmental care, and positioning himself as the architect of a new post-Cold-War economic order, just as John Maynard Keynes was of the last sixty years. This looks like strategic leadership for me, on the sort of multi-levelled scale that is needed.

Assuming all this is genuine, success will depend on how many people in leadership roles are able to do the *togetherness* bit - the holistic thinking that is second nature to *Resurgence* readers but rare elsewhere. Government departments are unlikely to merge in the near future, and it will be a while before the humanities and sciences in our schools, colleges and universities get into a creative huddle. So leadership for the 21st century will be about what some people call 'strategic adaptive leadership': the capacity to design and manage big complex change until Brown's "new synthesis" (aka sustainable development) becomes a reality - *despite* inhospitable structures and institutions.

How long do I think this will take? With the right leadership in the green movement and in government, about forty years - hope to see you at the party!

Sara Parkin is a Founder Director and Trustee of Forum for the Future, the sustainable development charity. She contributed to the development of Green Parties worldwide, playing various roles that include leading the UK Green Party and the European Greens during the 1970s and 1980s. In 2001 she was awarded an OBE for services to education and sustainable development.

THE AGENT OF CONSCIOUSNESS
LINDSAY CLARKE

REVALUING THE NOVEL

I believe that the art is to be as open as possible
to the intelligence of the Earth, reaching us
through our senses, our intuitions, our dreams.

I'VE JUST RETURNED from a working week under the hump-
backed thatch at Totleigh Barton in Devon, UK, where I was teaching
an Arvon Foundation course on writing fiction. At the end of the
week sixteen more people went away strengthened in their desire to
make their names as writers, and the continuing appeal of such
courses, along with the proliferation of creative writing programmes
across the land, suggests that thousands more share their ambition.
Clearly only a few stand much chance of success, yet the enthusiasm
generated is so impressive that the question arises as to why the need
to write should be so widespread now. Perhaps we should also be
asking what values we imagine we are serving when we take up the
difficult challenge of writing a novel.

Part of the answer must lie in the unprecedented quest for individuation that has gathered force over the last forty years as increasing numbers of people have felt the need for a greater degree of self-knowledge and self-determination. It's through language that we strive to open a passage from feeling into meaning, and imaginative writing can offer a lively way to explore fresh perspectives on how we see the world and our place within it. Whether the results get published or not, such an effort of discovery constitutes an important value in itself, yielding many satisfactions and subtle pleasures, and for some people that is already enough. But most participants on these courses hope for the rewards that may come from public recognition of their work, and to count themselves among that curious species of human being - the writers.

These were certainly my own, less than half-understood aspirations when I first felt the fire to write burning in my belly many years ago; but it wasn't long before I discovered that, far from the romantic image I had cherished, the writing life was that of a drudge sitting alone in a room for hour after hour, day in, day out, beating his brows while doubts did their best to silence him. Being a writer meant being a re-writer, reworking the material over and over again till a pattern of words emerged with something close to the quick of life moving through its cadences. Not, I imagine, the way most people would choose to spend their days, and if an aura of romance still hangs around the novelist's role it's perhaps a hankering after some illusory bohemia or, more profitably, an heirloom of a time more than a century ago when such champions of the imagination as Dickens, George Eliot, Balzac and Tolstoy were widely revered as Western culture's principal agents of consciousness.

But those authors thrived in a more coherent age than ours, an era before Freud, relativity theory and quantum uncertainties, when it was still feasible for their generous imaginations to convey with magisterial intelligence both the inward lives and outward behaviour of diverse characters along with a shrewd understanding of the social forces that shaped their destinies. By contrast, our own fissive and turbulent age so speedily out-trumps the novelist's imagination at every outrageous turn that J. G. Ballard insists that, "in a sense, the writer knows nothing any longer. He has no moral stance ... All he can do is devise various hypotheses and test them against the facts."

Yet earlier in the same essay, Ballard declared that "we live in a world ruled by fictions of every kind - mass-merchandising, advertising, politics conducted as a branch of advertising, the pre-empting of any original response to experience by the television screen." In such circumstances what *are* the facts against which 'hypotheses' can be tested; and what kind of values can novelists hope to celebrate or investigate each time they choose to add a story to the enormous novel in which we live these days? Or to put it another way, is the art of the novel now reduced to an attempt to articulate the relative truth of private experience over the spin and jangle of the times, or does some larger, more unifying vision remain possible?

IT'S CERTAINLY THE case that, in the absence of any myth that carries general authority, all serious writers have to answer such questions for themselves, and my own working life has largely been shaped by them. Like many educated young men of my generation I grew up in thrall to the gravely sceptical, all but nihilistic vision of the existentialist writers. What other stance held any dignity, one wondered, over against the atrocious facts of the Holocaust, nuclear weaponry, and the age-old history of religious conflict? A clear-eyed, tough-minded atheism calmly confronting the absurdity of existence with its own intellectual poise seemed the mark of a truly adult consciousness. Some version of that story still prevails in most serious contemporary fiction, but as I see things now, I was lucky not to become that kind of novelist before life took me by the scruff of the neck and shook me into what I take to be a richer, less reductive view of things.

Briefly expressed, a temporary melt-down of the ego under intense personal pressure opened me up to intimations of the unitary nature of all being and to subtly enlarging frequencies of intelligence which had been jammed out of consideration by my previous, tightly managed model of how things are. Thereafter, though the claims of the ego would often close me in again, the terms on which I lived my life were irrevocably altered and the course of my work as a writer was determined by that change. All the novels I've written since then are attempts to dramatise as engagingly as I can the various ordeals of transformation by which we make the journey into larger consciousness, from ego to soul.

In particular I've been concerned with the trouble we men have in responding to the claims made by the feminine principle. For the deeper we enter into life the more we are confounded by its contradictory nature until we come awake to the possibility that only through the difficult reconciliation of contrary forces can something new begin to happen. Such reconciliations are accomplished by an athletic exercise of imagination in both its inventive and ethical aspects, so it's in service of the imagination as a creative and compassionate value in itself that I try to write. The hope is that my fictions will contribute in an entertaining way to the emergence of a new mythology for our time.

FOR ME, THE imagination is the means by which we bring our experience of the outer world into negotiation with our inner world in order to create our personal myth of who we deeply are. The art is to keep the faculty as open as possible both ways, attending alertly to the intelligence reaching us through our senses and to the voices speaking through our dreams, our intuitions and the claims of conscience. A novel written in that reciprocating spirit may persuade a wider audience that, as Ted Hughes once said, "the laws of these two worlds are not contradictory at all: they are one inclusive system."

I know that my own best work gets done when I'm at my most receptive - more pipeline than engineer - listening for the words that enter the space briefly evacuated by the ego. Many writers have acknowledged the mysterious power of such inspiration as something that, in Emily Brontë's words, "strangely wills and works for itself". Increasingly I believe that the source is the living Earth itself, speaking to us through the imagination, urging us to live by better stories than are told by our desires for power and dominion.

True or not, I find it a fruitful tale to tell myself. My hope for the future of literature is that more writers find it works for them too, so that our words perform an ever richer and more conscious song of the Earth. And it may be that the stories we discover will encourage a more open and generous relationship to the delicate web that supports our life and invests it with a deeper sense of meaning.

Lindsay Clarke is the author of six novels, including The Chymical Wedding, *which won the Whitbread Fiction Prize. An Associate of the Creative Writing Programme at Cardiff University, he has taught in Ghana, the US and the UK, where he has also directed two Dartington Conferences and has been Scholar in Residence at Schumacher College. He regularly tutors both his own writing workshops in Bath and London and teaches writing courses for the Arvon Foundation and elsewhere at home and abroad.*

MAKING PEACE WITH GAIA

I believe that through our intelligence and
communication networks, human beings
are the nervous system of the planet.

THE IDEA THAT our planet is something special in the solar system and behaves as if it were alive came to me just over forty years
ago. This eureka moment was in September 1965 in California. Now,
it is becoming mainstream science and it goes far to explaining why
the Earth is in such an appalling state now. Let me go back to the
beginning. In 1961 I had just started working at the NASA Jet
Propulsion Laboratory (JPL) in California; my job was to invent
instruments to analyse the surface of the Moon and Mars. My NASA
colleagues were all busy building miniature and automated versions
of a bacteriology lab. Their intention was to send it to Mars where it
would sample the soil and try to grow the Martian micro-organisms

in culture media. They tested their equipment by letting it sample the soil of the nearby Mojave Desert, and it worked.

I could not help being somewhat sceptical and kept asking, "How do you know that bacteria on Mars will grow in your culture media? Or even that Martian life, if there is any, is anything at all like life here on Earth?" Naturally after a while they grew irritated with my scepticism and challenged me to offer an alternative. I said, why not look for an entropy reduction, for that surely is a characteristic of any form of life. This brought a mix of laughter and scorn because they could not envisage an apparatus that measured the entropy of Martian soil. They saw my questions as facetious and unhelpful. Actually I was quite serious.

But I had annoyed my colleagues more than I realised and shortly afterwards I was summoned to the office of the lab director, a formidable character named Bob Maghreblian. His first question was, "Why have you been upsetting our life detection team, with impractical proposals?" I answered, "I think they are wrong to assume that, if there is life on Mars, it will have evolved along the same path as here; their life detectors are good for Earth life, but not necessarily for alien life. What I propose instead is to look for some property of the whole planet that reveals a reduction of entropy" - in other words, a departure from the expected equilibrium state of a dead planet. This recipe for life detection drew on the ideas expressed by that outstanding physicist Schrödinger, who said in his small book *What is Life?* that entropy reduction is a singular characteristic of life. Maghreblian said, "Yes, but how would you make an entropy reduction detector?" I asked for time to think and he replied, "You have until Friday to bring me a sensible proposal on how to measure an entropy reduction on Mars."

I had two days to find the answer and, as Dr Johnson said, nothing concentrates the mind more than the prospect of hanging. I knew that if I failed to produce by Friday my chance of a new contract with NASA was small.

The answer came to me quite suddenly on the Thursday. The entropy of a planet like Mars can easily be found by measuring the chemical composition of its atmosphere and then making a few simple thermodynamic calculations. If the atmosphere is far from chemical and physical equilibrium - as is the Earth's atmosphere - this indicates low entropy and the presence of life. The way this happens is fairly simple. Life on the surface uses the mobile medium of air as a source of raw materials and a place to dispose of waste products. Doing this alters the composition in a way that reduces its entropy.

When I explained this idea to the JPL boss on the Friday he grew enthusiastic and asked me to submit a paper on the idea to one of the science journals and to start thinking about the hardware that would be needed. It was in fact published in *Nature* in 1965. Interestingly, its publication did nothing to improve my relationships with the biologists.

IN SEPTEMBER 1965, I was back at the JPL and in a small office that I shared with the astronomer Carl Sagan and my colleague Dian Hitchcock, a philosopher. Suddenly the door burst open and another astronomer, Lou Kaplan, entered with a pile of data sheets in his arms. They were from an infrared telescope at the Pic du Midi observatory in France, and they were the chemical compositions of the atmospheres of Mars and Venus. Both planets, Kaplan said, had atmospheres made almost entirely of carbon dioxide with only traces of oxygen and nitrogen present. According to my interpretation both planetary atmospheres were therefore close to chemical equilibrium and consequently Mars and Venus were lifeless.

This was not a popular conclusion for my employer NASA, for nothing then - as now - was such a good fundraiser as the prospect of finding alien life. It also meant that I had wasted time designing a gas chromatograph to analyse the Martian air. But then an awesome thought came into my mind. How does our own atmosphere, which is made of reactive gases at deep chemical disequilibrium, stay constant and breathable? Geological evidence and the fossil record suggest that it has been stable in composition for tens of millions of years. It seemed to me that the air was dynamically stable like our blood plasma, but that meant there must be regulation. Could it be that life at the surface kept the atmosphere in a constant but habitable state? I knew that most of the gases of the air were either a direct biological product like oxygen or else massively changed by the presence of life.

When I blurted these ideas out my friends were unmoved. Sagan said, "I don't believe the Earth regulates itself, but there's one thing that supports your idea and that is the properties of the Sun. Our star has warmed up by 30% since it began 4.5 billion years ago. Astronomers have sought to find an explanation of how the Earth kept a more or less constant temperature in spite of solar warming."

It then occurred to me that life must have been regulating the composition of the air for most of its existence; and of course we have now discovered through global warming that even a slight change of atmospheric composition affects the climate. I wondered, was this how life regulated the climate?

When I returned to England a few days later it was to my home in the village of Bowerchalke in Wiltshire. A near neighbour and friend was the author William Golding. He asked about my latest encounters with NASA and when I told him my idea he grew excited and said, "You must give it a proper name - I suggest you call your hypothesis Gaia, after the ancient Greek goddess of the Earth."

FROM THAT MOMENT in 1965 I have been guided by Gaia Theory and have tested its predictions. Scientists judge a theory, not by debating it, but by seeing how good its predictions are. Gaia has done well in this respect and has made more than ten predictions, most of which have been tested and found true. Some of its predictions, such as the one that clouds over the world oceans owe their abundance and density to the algae living in the surface waters, have led to the employment of thousands worldwide.

Since life began 3.5 billion years ago, the Earth has always been habitable despite the increase in solar luminosity. It might seem that climate regulation is poor if ice ages and warm periods occur at frequent intervals. In fact, during the last 2 to 3 million years the core surface region of the Earth, which lies between latitudes 45°N and 45°S, and includes 70% of the surface, has stayed comfortably habitable during both glaciations and interglacials like now. The temperature range was less than 5 degrees. This is not feeble regulation: it is just as good as we ourselves manage and is all that is needed. We regulate our bodies at the higher temperature of 37°C but over the same range of 5°C. We think of an ice age as a diminished state, but this is just an illusion because we prefer to live mostly in the North temperate regions outside the core. During the last glaciation there was considerably more life on Earth than there is now, so from a planetary viewpoint the cooler state was healthier. In a similar way the hot state that the Earth may soon be in will have less life than now. It is often stated that the Earth is just at the right distance from the Sun for life. This is nonsense: were it not for the regulation made possible by the presence of life, the Earth would be a hot waterless desert with a carbon dioxide atmosphere and a surface temperature of more than 60°C - a near interpolation between Mars and Venus.

Large ideas in science take about forty years to be accepted. They have to be fought over and tested and preferably expressed also in mathematics. As you probably know, Gaia Theory has had some fierce battles, especially with biologists such as Richard Dawkins. They were painful at the time but I am grateful to my opponents, for they sharpened the theory. They were right to object to my idea that life regulates the Earth, and their criticism made me realise that the regulation came from the whole system, life and the material environment, tightly coupled as the single entity, Gaia. The theory is now widely accepted as describing the Earth. In 2001, at a huge meeting in Amsterdam of all branches of science, more than a thousand delegates signed a declaration that stated as its first point: "The Earth is a self-regulating system made up from all life, including humans, and from the oceans, the atmosphere and the surface rocks."

At last Gaia theory was part of science but, sadly, it was about twenty years too late. If we had accepted in, say, 1980 that the Earth was in effect alive, we would have known that we cannot pollute the air and use the Earth's skin - its forest ecosystems - as a mere source of products to feed ourselves and furnish our homes. Those ecosystems, before we destroyed them, were regulating the climate and atmospheric composition. Our planet is now at a state that in medicine would be called 'failure'. It is at a crisis point beyond which it will soon move to a different stable state where it can more easily maintain itself physiologically. Gaia is normally healthy but in its three-and-a-half-billion-year life it has suffered from fevers several times before - the last was 55 million years ago at the beginning of the period the geologists call the Eocene.

At that time an accidental geological event released into the air between 1 and 2 million million tons of carbon dioxide. We are fairly sure about this from measurements made by Henry Elderfield of Cambridge University and his colleagues. They measured the carbon and oxygen isotopes of the sedimentary rocks of that time and confirmed the quantity of carbon put into the air and the extent the temperature changed. Putting this much CO_2 into the air caused the temperature of the temperate and Arctic regions to rise by 8°C and of the tropics by 5°C and it took about 200,000 years for conditions to return to the state before the fever. In the 20th century we released by burning fossil fuel about half that amount of CO_2 and if we continue as we are, we also will have released in thirty years from now more than a million million tons of CO_2. Moreover, the Sun is now hotter than it was 55 million years ago and we have disabled about 40% of Gaia's regulatory capacity by using land to feed people. This is why climate scientists are so concerned that we have caused irreversible climate change.

With the Earth's climate in net positive feedback it is not surprising that global warming is turning out to be much more serious than we thought only a few years ago. Systems in positive feedback act as amplifiers and any heating effect will be greater than predicted by classical climatology; and there is the danger of instability, something that will lead to surprises - events more deadly than we had imagined. There has been one already: the summer of 2003 in Europe, when more than 30,000 people died from the heat.

THE SIGNS ARE that we do not have long to act before global warming starts the irreversible move to much higher temperatures. In the recent BBC Horizon programme, Peter Cox of the Hadley Centre introduced the concept of global dimming. He presented evidence to suggest that the widespread haze of smog from cars and industry covered the Northern hemisphere and largely offset the global warming. The residence time of smog particles is only a few days, whereas that of carbon dioxide is about 100 years. Any economic downturn or planned cutback in fossil-fuel use that lessened the smog could carry us beyond the threshold of irreversible change. If it does there will be vast geographic as well as climatic changes. In many ways we live in a fool's climate. We are damned if we do and damned if we don't.

In no way do I mean that there is no hope for us or that there is nothing that we can do. I see our predicament as like that of the UK in 1940 when it was about to be invaded by a powerful enemy. We will do our best to avoid a catastrophe, but sadly in the present world the green concepts of sustainable development and renewable energy that inspired the Kyoto agreement are too late. They might have worked fifty years ago but now they are false and beguiling dreams that can only lead to failure. I cannot see the United States or the emerging economies of China and India, who are the main sources of emissions, cutting back in time. I fear that the worst may happen and our survivors will have to adapt to a hot and uncomfortable world. To retain civilisation they will need more than ever a secure and reliable source of energy to power the adaptation. Any large city would die in a week without electricity; all the services we take for granted depend on it, and this is why we need the security of a pow- ered descent - and for that I believe that there is no sensible alterna- tive to nuclear energy.

Long overdue is a change in the way we think about the Earth. We have to stop thinking that we are in charge and are the stewards of the Earth. We have to abandon the idea that the only thing that matters is the welfare of humankind and that the Earth was given to us for our benefit alone. We have for too long behaved badly towards the host of other life forms with which we share our planet and on whom we depend for a habitable environment. Although we pay lip-service to threats to wildlife and to ecosystems like coral reefs, the Amazon forests, and the fresh-water ecosystems here in the UK, we are in practice obsessed with environmental hazards to personal health such as pesticide residues in foodstuff, nuclear radiation, and genetically modified food. And to judge from the supermarket shelves, we seem to have the illusion that if the whole planet were farmed organically all would be well. To the contrary: I think it extremely unlikely that the regulatory functions of natural ecosystems can simply be replaced by farmland.

Perhaps the saddest thing is that if we fail, Gaia will lose as much as or more than we do. Not only will wildlife and whole ecosystems become extinct, but in human civilisation the planet has a precious resource. We are not merely a disease: we are through our intelligence and communication the nervous system of the planet. Through us Gaia has seen herself from space and seen how beautiful she is, and she begins to know her place in the universe. We should be the heart and mind of the Earth, not its malady. So let us be brave and cease thinking of human needs and rights alone and see that we have harmed the living Earth and need to make our peace with Gaia. We must do it while we are still strong enough to negotiate and not a broken rabble led by brutal warlords. Most of all we should remember that we are a part of it and it is indeed our home.

James Lovelock is an independent scientist, environmentalist, author and researcher. He is the author of The Gaia Theory, The Ages of Gaia, Homage to Gaia, *and* Revenge of Gaia. *He invented the electron capture detector, which revealed the ubiquitous distribution of pesticide residues and prompted Rachel Carson to write her book* Silent Spring. *The instrument was later used to discover and measure the abundance of polychlorinated biphenyls (PCBs), chlorofluorocarbons (CFCs) and nitrous oxide in the atmosphere.*

JOINING UP THE DOTS

If we think holistically about our planetary
problems, we are presented with
an equal number of solutions.

IT IS NOW well over thirty years since a bunch of young idealists colonised a derelict slate quarry in Wales to establish the Centre for Alternative Technology. At that time what we meant by 'being green' was a lot less defined, and certainly a lot less tested. The original pioneers were inspired by the notion of building a living community to test ideas for self-sufficient living, to discover which ones worked and which ones didn't. Back in the early 1970s, the key motive was to develop ways of surviving the collapse of society. It was the height of the Cold War, and many people thought a full-out nuclear exchange was likely, if not inevitable. If not nuclear war, then some biological or ecological disaster fuelled a feeling of imminent collapse, so we felt it necessary to 'take to the hills' and develop self-reliant technologies.

Three decades later, such a collapse has still not happened. However, after the long sleep of the 1980s and 1990s, the fears of these original pioneers are now re-emerging. We now depend for our continued existence on increasingly remote suppliers working through ever more distant systems that have no obligations to us, and indeed are not expected to have any; and all this totally reliant on easy access to cheap, abundant fossil fuels. With escalating global demand for diminishing fossil-fuel reserves, we are once again forced to question which aspects of our lives we should trust to transnational corporations and which aspects are better sourced more locally.

SO WHAT HAVE we learned in forty years? Well, we must recognise that we 'greens' have successfully identified and publicised a great many ecological challenges. So much so, that I feel our task in coming decades is to re-focus our resources, and indeed the world's resources, on solving the urgent, critical challenges and not be distracted by the peripheral ones. By 'urgent challenges', I mean those which are irreversible, or could run away out of control, or are an absolute moral imperative. My choice would be

- Energy (climate change and peak oil)
- Biodiversity and habitat
- Global equity

This trinity poses a formidable challenge to the security and wellbeing of everyone on Earth. Runaway climate change would dwarf Hurricane Katrina and continue for tens of thousands of years. Also, our oil- and gas-powered economies are now being halted by the

139

immovable facts of geology - despite accelerating demand, global rates of production may be approaching their peak. In addition, biodiversity is vital as it gives stability to the biosphere and species extinctions are, of course, irreversible. And despite record increases in global economic activity, the world's rich are still getting richer and the poor are still getting poorer.

Although these three challenges are becoming increasingly familiar, their experts still work in relative isolation and their solutions are rarely considered holistically. The key to success will be to recognise that these problems and therefore their solutions are fundamentally and inextricably linked. There are solutions to peak oil that accelerate climate change, and there are solutions to global equity that exacerbate peak oil. Solving one challenge at the expense of another will not do. We must solve them together. Indeed, once we join the dots and look for the bigger picture, we find plenty of common ground. Facing up to our oil addiction and re-thinking our diet, buildings, energy, water, work, clothing, heating, holidays and health care can mitigate climate change, help preserve habitat and release resources the majority world urgently needs.

But even if we in the UK can get our carbon emissions under control, humanity can only avoid catastrophic conflict, climate chaos or devastation of habitat if we can encourage everyone else to follow suit. A 'global solution' must embrace all our needs. The major contender, contraction and convergence, suggests that we in the overdeveloped West must contract our level of emissions to converge at some 'fair share' with those of the majority world, thus working towards equity between North and South.

Our current use of fossil fuels has grown well above that which is required to deliver our wellbeing; we are, in fact, energy-obese. A 'powerdown plus renewables' strategy will not only reduce and forestall the problems: it will also make us much better-placed to cope with them. For example, the potential powerdown that could be achieved through a rethink in the way we grow and distribute our food is massive. We export many thousands of tonnes of lamb to the EU whilst importing a very similar amount of lamb from the EU. Similar paradoxes exist for almost everything we buy. Local food solutions are not only more energy-efficient: they are considerably more reliable.

Once we have contracted our energy consumption to converge with our fair share, delivering it with renewable sources not only becomes achievable but it rapidly becomes cheaper as oil prices hit the roof, and potentially more dependable as fossil-fuel imports become intermittent. Solving these three challenges holds the potential to allow us to create the kind of world that we actually want to live in. It doesn't have to be a huge disaster. We now have a chance to change everything, because everything must be changed. But we must use the time and the oil we have left to the very best effect now and not bury our heads in the sands of denial.

PERHAPS THE NEXT KEY lesson for the coming forty years is that the environmental movement cannot simply project an array of scary disasters and expect that society will 'hear the message' and make the changes required. We must actively engage global society in a solutions-driven programme. But in doing this we must all 'walk our talk'. The choices we make in the UK will set trends that will be followed by many others. For example, if Britain makes nuclear power a core component of its response to climate change and energy security, many other rapidly developing economies will want to follow suit. It will then be very hard for us to make a case for why we are allowed civil nuclear power when it is forbidden to others.

Another important lesson is to recognise that the current 'development' strategy of encouraging the majority world to pull itself out of poverty through globalised trade could well be a blind alley. The sheer scale of such an enterprise may prove more than the planet's climate can bear, and there probably isn't enough cheap oil left to do it for long enough. Far better, if we enable the majority world to become self-reliant.

I feel that we must also recognise that alternative lifestyles and alternative personal aspirations are just as important as alternative technologies. As well as reducing our impacts, they engage people by fulfilling needs that are currently going unsatisfied. Our energy-intensive, consumerist lifestyles are not actually making us any happier. Since the 1970s the UK's GDP (gross domestic product) has doubled, but our perceived 'satisfaction with life' has hardly changed.

I would say the most important thing we have learned is to keep up the pressure; although the global challenges seem very large, powerful and daunting, things are changing - and they're changing fast!

Paul Allen is Development Director at the Centre for Alternative Technology in Wales. He was previously Director of EcoDyfi and Dulas Engineering, companies which specialised in designing renewable energy systems. He writes extensively on sustainable development issues.

THE PEACEMAKER
SCILLA ELWORTHY

INVESTING IN HEALING

We have had 100 years of war and peace - but
what have we learned?

W HEN I WAS thirteen I watched on a grainy black and
white TV as kids my age threw themselves at Soviet tanks rolling into
Budapest to crush the Hungarian uprising. I rushed upstairs to pack
my things to go and join them. My mother told me not to be so silly.

That was half a century ago. What have we learned since then
about dealing with terror, with enemies or with dictators? Has the
very nature of war changed? What do we now know about resolving
conflict that we didn't know then? And how does that tell us to prepare for the next fifty years?

The Cold War

The most ominous conflict in the last half of the 20th century was
the ill-named Cold War. At its height, in its heat, it consumed

143

unimaginable amounts of money, skill and energy. Margaret Thatcher, Ronald Reagan and Leonid Brezhnev built up their nuclear arsenals to the point at which every person on the planet could be destroyed three times.

In the summer of 1982 I was in New York to lobby delegates at the UN Second Special Session on Disarmament, getting increasingly depressed by the sterility of the proceedings. Then I went to Central Park for a demonstration against nuclear weapons; a million people turned up, the whole day was noisy and entirely peaceful, and even New York cops ended up with badges all down their ties. "This", I thought, "will change things."

Wrong. The next day, back in the UN building, absolutely nothing changed. Dispirited, I was strap-hanging on a tram on Broadway when I suddenly had the thought: What if all these passionate people in the streets could talk, one-to-one, with the people who actually make decisions on nuclear weapons - in the weapons laboratories, the ministries, the intelligence and military services? Little did I know that this thought was going to keep me busy for twenty-five years! I came home and set up a research group - soon called the Oxford Research Group - round my kitchen table.

First we had to find out who were the people who make decisions on nuclear weapons, in the UK, China, Russia, France and the US. We had to draw up 'wiring diagrams' tracing how, in each country, the warhead designers connected with military intelligence and with the contractors who build the 'platforms' from which they are fired. Who signed the cheques? Did politicians give the initial authorisation? Where did the whole process start?

The establishment did not like us delving into these questions of accountability, particularly in France, where men in raincoats and trilby hats followed our researcher about, broke into his flat and stole his data. One day when I took my car to the garage I discovered that the tyres had been cut around the inside and would have burst at speed.

After three years we began talking to church groups, peace groups, women's groups and others who wanted to do something more in their opposition to nuclear weapons than simply protest. We were offering them the possibility of 'adopting' one policy-maker in the UK and that person's opposite number in China. We emphasised the necessity of a nonconfrontational approach, because from experience we knew that if you are full of anger when you write or talk to someone you will get nowhere.

After a pilot project and a gradual build-up, there were some eighty groups in the UK, plus some in the US and Scandinavia, all trying to open a dialogue. Some never got a reply to their first, painstakingly composed letter. One heard nothing over a period of four years, and then their man was elevated to the peerage and in his maiden speech to the House of Lords used all their arguments against nuclear weapons! Some eventually got to meet their correspondent and talk. Even, in one case, in China.

"You young women who don't know anything about war"
Let me give another example of the power of dialogue. In the mid-1980s the Cold War between East and West had heated up with the deployment, by both sides, of new short-range nuclear missiles in central Europe. In 1986 a group of women who were tired of the polarisation and the millions of tax dollars being poured into armaments decided to go to the NATO headquarters in Brussels and talk to decision-makers there about it.

NATO was then a military alliance of Western nations, controlling thousands of nuclear weapons. The women were mostly members of their national parliaments, representatives of women's organisations or women who had researched the military industry. Despite the fact that we were knowledgeable, non-combative and well-known in our own countries (one was the wife of a president), we had the greatest difficulty getting appointments. It took a year, and a petition from members of the European Parliament, to persuade the NATO Secretary General that he had nothing to lose by talking to us.

Finally, in June 1987 we were allowed into the headquarters: the first women, other than secretaries, cleaners and Thatcher to cross the threshold. We met the generals and ambassadors representing our own nations, and the Secretary General, then Lord Carrington. He referred to us as "you young women who don't know anything about war".

We were deeply alarmed by what we found: that no channel of communication existed between NATO and the Warsaw Pact, and that NATO took decisions that were not even *reported* to the parliaments of the member countries for months or even years, let alone debated. We started to speak out clearly about this in our own countries. And we got results. A channel of communication between NATO and the Warsaw Pact was set up. A television documentary about the lack of parliamentary debate of NATO decisions was made and shown on British television.

Baghdad, January 2003
Three months before the invasion of Iraq, I went there with the former First Lady of Greece and the former UN Humanitarian Co-ordinator in Iraq to do what we could to find ways to avert war. We met with the Deputy Prime Minister, the Foreign Minister and the Oil Minister and talked with doctors, teachers and scientists.

We visited the Foot-and-Mouth Disease Institute which was high on the list in the UK Government dossier (published October 2002) of sites at which biological weapons were being made. Since 1994 the site had been inspected sixty times, it had been closed since 1995, and there were cameras everywhere connected to the Baghdad Monitoring Centre of UNSCOM (United Nations Special Commission). The place was wrecked. It was painful to have the British Prime Minister still insisting it was a threat.

On our return we sent Tony Blair a seven-point plan for averting war. He reportedly glanced at it and said, "Oh, I know all that." We now know that he had committed the UK to support the US invasion as many as five months previously.

So, what of today?

The Iraq war is now into its fourth year, with no end in sight. In the global war on terror, of which Iraq is a core part in George W. Bush's worldview, at least 90,000 people have been detained without trial; torture, rendition and prisoner abuse are widespread. Anti-Americanism, across the Islamic world in particular, has reached explosive levels.

This hardly adds up to a spectacular success for the conduct of the war on terror, even as its proponents insist that it is unavoidable. This view is part of a neo-conservative belief that the Western security paradigm has to be based on keeping control of a fractured and disparate world. In this analysis, military power is the only option.

Very senior members of the British military do not agree with this. General Sir Rupert Smith argues that over the past fifteen years both the Western allies and the Russians have entered into a series of military engagements that have spectacularly failed to achieve the results intended.

What are the options?

Preventing war works on the same principle as inoculation for small-pox - it has to be done methodically, with proven vaccines, and as a fundamental, properly funded policy. The UK currently allocates to conflict prevention and resolution less than 0.5% of the funding allocated for military intervention - and the UK has a better record in this than all except the Scandinavian countries.

The damage done to the fabric of society by any war has to be healed if a lasting peace is to be established. Reconstructing build-ings is the easy part. What is most difficult, and least attended to, are the deep wounds left in the minds and hearts of those who live on. Innocent people on all sides will have been killed, women raped, children made mute by the horrors they have witnessed, or left to manage stumps of limbs. Other children are yet to be blown to pieces by unexploded bombs.

If the resulting rage and grief are not addressed they will foment revenge and future terror and fester into further horror. That's why serious skill and serious money must be invested in this healing. It is why governments must be persuaded that the human factor - human security - rather than the use of force offers the best chance for peace in the 21st century. Persuading them is the job of the people: you and me.

Scilla Elworthy is founder of Peace Direct, which supports grassroots peacebuilding in conflict areas <www.peacedirect.org> and co-author with Gabrielle Rifkind of Making Terrorism History (Rider, 2006).

THE COUNTRYSIDE CRUSADER
FIONA REYNOLDS

A RURAL REPLAN

Communities of the past had a deep connection
with the land, and I believe they have much
to teach us about how we can
adapt to future changes.

I'M ONE OF millions of people in Britain for whom the country-side means an incalculable amount. I've lived north, south, east and west, and now that I'm lucky enough to have settled in the south Cotswolds I draw daily succour from the landscape around me. But it's much more than a physical connection - for me, there's a deep sense of historical continuity which is both profoundly significant, and increasingly important in a world that sometimes seems intent on forgetting the past and the lessons it has for our future.

But that's just my view of the countryside. As you would expect of something so central to the nation's psyche, the countryside appears in many guises. It is the creative spark of Wordsworth's vales and hills, or Blake's 'Jerusalem'. It is the object of affection for Ewan MacColl's working man, and an Eden-like inversion of the choking pollution of the cities for Robert Tressell's ragged-trousered philanthropist. For millions of people it's a place to escape to, to find physical refreshment. For millions more, it's home and workplace. And for everyone it's personal: 'countryside' is everything from heather moorland, rolling pasture, charming domestic architecture, contented-looking cattle, to dry-stone walls and soaring mountains.

Vibrant towns and cities are also important, but given such traditions and imagery it is hardly a surprise that the British love the countryside. Urban outmigration and rural house prices suggest that a large chunk of mainstream Britain longs for a retreat to a place where everyone knows their neighbours and there are ducks on the village green. Our countryside offers grounding, stability and reassurance. It offers permanence at a time of seemingly continuous change. And yet there has arguably never been more change in the countryside, nor a stronger imperative for more to come.

If our collective vision of the countryside is built upon myths of often distant heritage, the changes that it has seen over the last forty years have transformed the appearance of many rural areas. Farming remains by far the dominant land use, but while the total area of the UK under agriculture has remained relatively constant, yields have quadrupled. It has changed for people, too. In the second half of the 20th century agriculture accounted for a reasonably steady 2% of the economy. But in the same period there was a 65% decline in the number of farms, a 77% decrease in farm employment, and substantial decreases in habitat diversity and wildlife.

THE COUNTRYSIDE IS not what it used to be, but what has been the cause? Changes in farming are often blamed on politicians' understanding (or not) of the countryside. But the reasoned explanation for the changes that took place right across Western Europe is plain to see in the 1957 Treaty of Rome. National security required increased productivity, linked to a fair standard of living for the agricultural community, stabilised markets, and guaranteed supplies at reasonable prices. The response to post-war austerity was to totally restructure farming through financial assistance from the mid-1960s to the late 1970s. But by the time Britain joined the Common Market in the 1980s such policies had outstripped need. The creation of huge annual surpluses of the major farm commodities was described through countryside-inspired metaphors such as milk lakes and butter mountains.

Yet if the romantic vision of the countryside in the 1950s is a distant dream, today's realities are relegating the events of the over-producing 1980s to memory too. We have had almost a generation of bureaucratic attempts to resolve the relationship between farming and the environment, and some things are getting better. CAP reform means that at last farmers are being paid for delivering public benefits, not simply producing food. But the breakdown of our understanding of the countryside goes far beyond today's preoccupations with Single Farm Payments, supermarkets and avian flu.

The harsh reality is that, with few exceptions, we have forgotten what once we knew. We no longer consider how the distribution of natural resources has shaped our world and should shape it still. We teach our children business studies rather than geography. We plan with little consideration for variations in weather, river catchments and flood plains, forgetting or ignoring the insights and common sense of our ancestors, who knew and understood the land as we no longer do.

The results of this collective loss of memory and understanding could be catastrophic. Children who grow up with minimal contact with the countryside not only don't know where food comes from but have no sense of natural processes and our dependence on them. Successive generations' disregard for land form and natural resources mean that we have little understanding of how our lifestyles and decisions impact on our planet as well as on the local environment. Climate change, already with us, is both challenging what we have come to regard as 'the norm' and challenging us to accept that the future cannot be like the past. Resource poverty - communities with limited access to fresh water; with degraded soils and limited supplies of energy - will dictate a new policy language and response.

FOR ANYONE INVOLVED in the environmental movement, such prospects are sobering. And they call for a much more holistic view of change and both its threats and opportunities than we have hitherto taken. As it becomes impossible to protect species by creating nature reserves, to grow the crops we have become used to producing, or to plan for water without planning for limited water, we must learn to think as well as live in a different way.

At the same time as public support for the countryside and what it stands for is growing as never before, so it becomes ever more important to widen people's understanding of its importance, to think of it as a resource rather than a factory floor or playground. In a world challenged by climate change it is inconceivable to think that we won't need the productive capability of our land, and access to the resources of clean air, water, and productive soils it provides. But to utilise them intelligently will require new disciplines, with constraints on transport and energy and a new focus on localism in our approach.

This is where - to return to my opening remarks - history has something to teach us. Communities of the past were more connected with their localities: they understood what their soil could produce and what it could not, and which land flooded and which was better for building on, planting trees or grazing. Communities of the future will have to learn those skills again, within a new and more urgent need to limit our collective environmental footprint in the interests of a wider planet and future generations.

In this new world we will also need new skills: spatial approaches to planning and managing natural resources that work with environmental functions such as river catchments and coastal zones; landscape-scale nature conservation and energy-efficient production techniques. Green infrastructure - the supply of essential resources including access to places of beauty and significance - will be as important as physical infrastructure is today. And we will need to re-educate and re-engage people in how natural systems work, and how our interventions impact on them. We must offer the knowledge to understand and adapt to the forces of environmental change. And we will need to empower people to make choices which benefit the natural and cultural environment.

Today's rather romantic view of the countryside, often purveyed in magazines, cinema and lifestyle marketing is not, as we all know, the reality today. But we face a yet harder challenge in responding to tomorrow's challenges where our dependence, not only on the beauty of the countryside but on its physical resources, will once again feel closer to home. We would do well, then, to heed what a close reading of landscape history has always told us and always will: look at and learn from the past and it will help you meet the future.

Fiona Reynolds is Director General of the National Trust.

LEARNING FROM LEONARDO

In my view, what we need today is exactly the kind of science that Leonardo da Vinci outlined 500 years ago.

I HAVE BEEN fascinated by Leonardo da Vinci's science for over three decades, and over the years have referred to it in several of my writings, without, however, studying his extensive notebooks in any detail. The impetus to do so came in the mid-1990s, when I saw a large exhibition of Leonardo's drawings at the Queen's Gallery at Buckingham Palace in London. As I gazed at those magnificent drawings which juxtaposed architecture and human anatomy, turbulent water and turbulent air, water vortices, the flow of human hair and the growth patterns of grasses, I realised that Leonardo's systematic studies of living and non-living forms amounted to a science of quality and wholeness - fundamentally different from the mechanistic science of Galileo and Newton.

Having explored the modern counterparts to Leonardo's approach, known as complexity theory and systems theory, I felt that it was time for me to study Leonardo's notebooks in earnest and to evaluate his scientific thought from the perspective of the most recent advances in modern science. When I embarked on this project, I discovered that there are very few books on Leonardo's science, even though he left thousands of pages full of detailed descriptions of his experiments and long analyses of his findings. Moreover, most authors who have discussed Leonardo's scientific work have looked at it through Newtonian lenses, which has often prevented them from understanding its essential nature.

Only now, as the limits of Newtonian science are becoming all too apparent and the mechanistic Cartesian worldview is giving way to an organic and ecological view not unlike Leonardo's, can we begin to appreciate the full power of his science and its great relevance for our modern era. Studying Leonardo allows us to recognise his science as a solid body of knowledge, but also shows why it cannot be understood without his art, nor his art without the science.

WHEN THE YOUNG Leonardo received his training as painter, sculptor and engineer in Florence, the worldview of his contemporaries was still entangled in medieval thinking. Science in the modern sense, as a systematic empirical method for gaining knowledge about the natural world, did not exist. Knowledge about natural phenomena had been handed down by Aristotle and other philosophers of antiquity, and was fused with Christian doctrine by the Scholastic theologians who presented it as the officially authorised creed and condemned scientific experiments as subversive, seeing any attack on Aristotle's science as an attack on the Church. Leonardo broke with this tradition: "First I shall do some experiments before I proceed farther, because my intention is to cite experience first and then with reasoning show why such experience is bound to operate in such a way. And this is the true rule by which those who speculate about the effects of nature must proceed."

One hundred years before Galileo and Bacon, Leonardo single-handedly developed a new empirical approach, involving the systematic observation of nature, reasoning, and mathematics - in other words, the main characteristics of what is known today as the scientific method. He fully realised that he was breaking new ground. He humbly called himself *omo sanza lettere* ('an unlettered man'), but with some irony and with pride in his new method, seeing himself as an "interpreter between nature and humans".

Leonardo's approach to scientific knowledge was visual, and it was the approach of a painter. "Painting", he declared, "embraces within itself all the forms of nature." I believe that this statement is the key to understanding Leonardo's science. He asserts repeatedly that painting involves the study of natural forms, and he emphasises the intimate connection between the artistic representation of those forms and the intellectual understanding of their intrinsic nature.

Painting, for Leonardo, is both an art and a science - a science of natural forms, of qualities, quite different from the quantitative, mechanistic science that would emerge 200 years later. Leonardo's forms are living forms, continually shaped and transformed by underlying processes. Throughout his life he studied, drew and painted the rocks and sediments of the Earth, shaped by water; the growth of plants, shaped by their metabolism; and the anatomy of the animal body in motion.

Nature as a whole was alive for Leonardo, and he saw the patterns and processes in the macrocosm (the Earth) as being similar to those in the microcosm (the human body). At the most fundamental level, he always sought to understand the nature of life. Today, a new systemic understanding of life is emerging at the forefront of science - an understanding in terms of metabolic processes and their patterns of organisation; and those are precisely the phenomena which Leonardo explored throughout his life.

In the macrocosm, the main themes of Leonardo's science were the movements of water and air, the geological forms and transformations of the Earth, and the botanical diversity and growth patterns of plants. In the microcosm, his main focus was on the human body - its beauty and proportions, the mechanics of its movements, and how it compared to other animal bodies in motion.

Unlike Descartes, Leonardo never thought of the body as a machine, even though he was a brilliant engineer who designed countless machines and mechanical devices. "Nature cannot give movement to animals without mechanical instruments," he explained, but that did not imply for him that living organisms were machines. It only implied that, in order to understand the movements of the animal body, he needed to explore the principles of mechanics, which he did for many years in a thorough and systematic way. He clearly understood that the means of the body's movements were mechanical, but that their origin lay in the soul, the nature of which was not mechanical but spiritual.

Leonardo did not pursue science and engineering in order to dominate nature, as Francis Bacon did a century later. He had a deep respect for all life, a special compassion for animals, and great awe and reverence for nature's complexity and abundance. While being a brilliant inventor and designer himself, he always thought that nature's ingenuity was vastly superior to human design, and he felt that we would be wise to respect nature and learn from her. "Though human ingenuity in various inventions uses different instruments for the same end," he declared, "it will never discover an invention more beautiful, easier, or more economical than nature's, because in her inventions nothing is wanting and nothing is superfluous."

THIS ATTITUDE OF seeing nature as a model and mentor is now being rediscovered in the practice of ecological design. Like Leonardo 500 years ago, ecodesigners today study the patterns and flows in the natural world and try to incorporate the underlying principles into their design processes. Underlying such an attitude of appreciation and respect for nature is a philosophical stance that does not view humans as standing apart from the rest of the living world but rather as being fundamentally embedded in, and dependent upon, the entire community of life in the biosphere.

Leonardo's synthesis of art and science is infused with this deep ecological awareness. This is the reason why his legacy is relevant to our time. As we recognise that our sciences and technologies have become increasingly narrow in their focus, unable to understand our multi-faceted problems from an interdisciplinary perspective, and dominated by corporations more interested in financial rewards than in the wellbeing of humanity, we urgently need a science that honours and respects the unity of all life, recognises the fundamental interdependence of all natural phenomena, and reconnects us with the living Earth. What we need today is exactly the kind of science Leonardo da Vinci anticipated and outlined 500 years ago.

Fritjof Capra is a physicist and systems theorist and is the author of several international bestsellers including The Tao of Physics, The Web of Life *and* The Hidden Connections. *<www.fritjofcapra.net>*